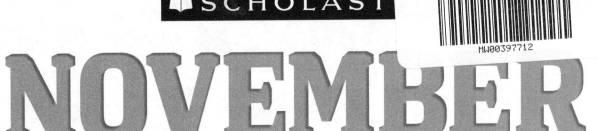

NOVEMBER
Monthly Idea Book

Ready-to-Use Templates, Activities, Management Tools, and More — for Every Day of the Month

Karen Sevaly

New York • Toronto • London • Auckland • Sydney
Mexico City • New Delhi • Hong Kong • Buenos Aires

Teaching *Resources*

DEDICATION

This book is dedicated to teachers and children everywhere.

Cover design by Maria Lilja
Cover art by Jillian Phillips
Interior design by Melinda Belter
Illustrations by Karen Sevaly

ISBN 978-0-545-37935-9

Text and illustrations © 2013 by Scholastic Inc.
All rights reserved.
Printed in the U.S.A.

1 2 3 4 5 6 7 8 9 10   40   19 18 17 16 15 14 13

CONTENTS

FAVORITE TOPICS

CONTENTS

STATES & CAPITALS

WOODLAND ANIMALS

· ·

REV UP FOR READING!

Reproducible Patterns

THANKSGIVING: HISTORY AND HARVEST

Reproducible Patterns

TURKEY TIME!

Reproducible Patterns

AWARDS, INCENTIVES, AND MORE

Reproducible Patterns

ANSWER KEY

INTRODUCTION

Welcome to the original monthly idea book series! This book was written especially for teachers getting ready to teach topics related to the month of November.

Each book in this month-by-month series is filled with dozens of ideas for PreK–3 classrooms. Activities connect to the Common Core State Standards for Reading (Foundational Skills), among other subjects, to help you meet the needs of your students. (See page 16.)

Most everything you need to prepare the lessons and activities in this resource are included, such as:

- calendar and weather-related props
- book cover patterns and stationery for writing assignments
- reproducible booklet patterns
- games that support learning in curriculum areas such as math, science, and writing
- activity sheets that help students organize information, respond to learning, and explore topics in a meaningful way
- reproducible patterns for projects that connect to holidays, special occasions, and commemorative events

All year long, you can weave the activities in these unique books into your monthly lesson plans and classroom activities. Happy teaching!

What's Inside

You'll find that this book is chock-full of reproducibles that make lesson planning easier:

■ puppets and
   picture props

■ bookmarks,
   booklets, and
   book covers

■ game boards,
   puzzles, and
   word finds

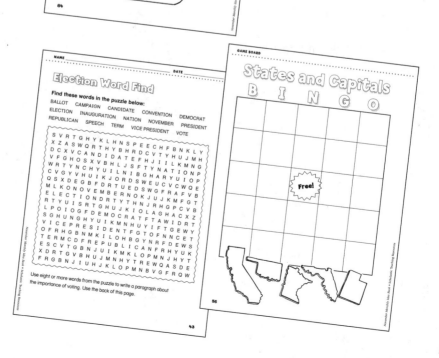

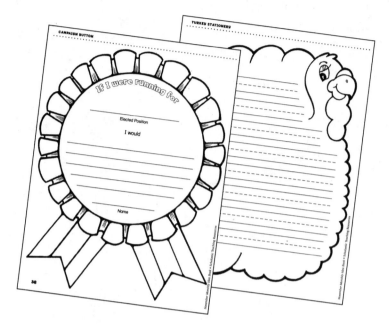

■ stationery

■ awards and certificates

How to Use This Book

The reproducible pages in this book have flexible use and may be modified to meet your particular classroom needs. Use the reproducible activity pages and patterns in conjunction with the suggested activities or weave them into your curriculum in other ways.

★ PHOTOCOPY OR SCAN

To get started, think about your developing lesson plans and upcoming bulletin boards. If desired, carefully remove the pages you will need. Duplicate those pages on copy paper, color paper, tagboard, or overhead transparency sheets. If you have access to a scanner, consider saving the pattern pages as PDF files. That way, you can size images up or down and customize them with text to create individualized lessons, center-time activities, interactive whiteboard lessons, homework pages, and more.

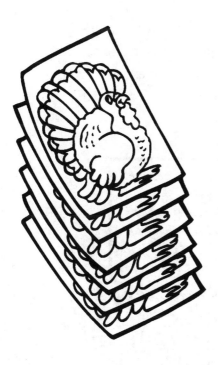

★ LAMINATE FOR DURABILITY

Laminating the reproducibles will help you extend their use. If you have access to a roll laminator, then you already know how fortunate you are when it comes to saving time and resources. If you don't have a laminator, clear adhesive vinyl covering works well. Just sandwich the pattern between two sheets of vinyl and cut off any excess. Then try some of these ideas:

- Put laminated sheets of stationery in a writing center to use for handwriting practice. Wipe-off markers work great on coated pages and can easily be erased with dry tissue.

- Add longevity to calendars, weather-related pictures, and pocket chart rebus pictures by preserving them with lamination.

- Transform picture props into flannel board figures. After lamination, add a tab of hook-and-loop fastener to the back of the props and invite students to adhere them to the flannel board for storytelling fun.

- To enliven magnet board activities, affix sections of magnet tape to the back of the picture props. Then encourage students to sort images according to the skills you're working on. For example, you might have them group images by commonalities such as initial sound, habitat, or physical attributes.

★ BULLETIN BOARDS

1. Set the Stage

Use background paper colors that complement many themes and seasons. For example, the dark background you used as a spooky display in October will have dramatic effect in November, when you begin a unit on woodland animals or Thanksgiving.

While paper works well, there are other background options available. You might also try fabric from a colorful bed sheet or gingham material. Discontinued rolls of patterned wallpaper can be purchased at discount stores. What's more, newspapers are easy to use and readily available. Attach a background of comics to set off a lesson on riddles, or use grocery store flyers to provide food for thought on a bulletin board about nutrition.

2. Make the Display

The reproducible patterns in this book can be enlarged to fit your needs. When we say enlarge, we mean it! Think BIG! Use an overhead projector to enlarge the images you need to make your bulletin board extraordinary.

If your school has a stencil press, you're lucky. The rest of us can use these strategies for making headers and titles.

- Cut strips of paper, cloud shapes, or cartoon bubbles. They will all look great! Then, by hand, write the text using wide-tipped permanent markers or tempera paint.

- If you must cut individual letters, use 4- by 6-inch pieces of construction paper. (Laminate first, if you can.) Cut the uppercase letters as shown on page 14. No need to measure, as somewhat irregular letters will look creative, not messy.

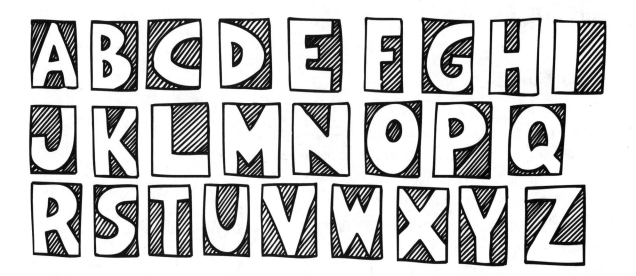

ABCDE FGHI
JKLMN OPQ
RSTUVWXYZ

3. Add Color and Embellishments

Use your imagination! You'll be surprised at the great displays you can create.

- Watercolor markers work great on small areas. On larger areas, you can switch to crayons, color chalk, or pastels. (Lamination will keep the color off of you. No laminator? A little hairspray will do the trick as a fixative.)

- Cut character eyes and teeth from white paper and glue them in place. The features will really stand out and make your bulletin boards engaging.

- For special effects, include items that provide texture and visual interest, such as buttons, yarn, and lace. Try cellophane or blue glitter glue on water scenes. Consider using metallic wrapping paper or aluminum foil to add a bit of shimmer to stars and belt buckles.

- Finally, take a picture of your completed bulletin board. Store the photos in a recipe box or large sturdy envelope. Next year when you want to create the same display, you'll know right where everything goes. You might even want to supply students with pushpins and invite them to recreate the display, following your directions and using the photograph as support.

Staying Organized

Organizing materials with monthly file folders provides
you with a location to save reproducible activity pages and
patterns, along with related craft ideas, recipes, and magazine
or periodical articles.

If you prefer, use file boxes instead of folders. You'll find
that with boxes there will plenty of room to store enlarged
patterns, sample art projects, bulletin board materials, and
much more.

Meeting the Standards

CONNECTIONS TO THE COMMON CORE STATE STANDARDS

The Common Core State Standards Initiative (CCSSI) has outlined learning expectations in English/Language Arts, among other subject areas, for students at different grade levels. In general, the activities in this book align with the following standards for students in grades K–3. For more information, visit the CCSSI website at www.corestandards.org.

Reading: Foundational Skills

Print Concepts

- RF.K.1, RF.1.1. Demonstrate understanding of the organization and basic features of print.

Phonics and Word Recognition

- RF.K.3, RF.1.3, RF.2.3, RF.3.3. Know and apply grade-level phonics and word analysis skills in decoding words.

Fluency

- RF.K.4. Read emergent-reader texts with purpose and understanding.

- RF.1.4, RF.2.4, RF.3.4. Read with sufficient accuracy and fluency to support comprehension.

Writing

Production and Distribution of Writing

- W.3.4. Produce writing in which the development and organization are appropriate to task and purpose.

- W.K.5, W.1.5, W.2.5, W.3.5. Focus on a topic and strengthen writing as needed by revising and editing.

Research to Build and Present Knowledge

- W.K.7, W.1.7, W.2.7. Participate in shared research and writing projects.

- W.3.7. Conduct short research projects that build knowledge about a topic.

- W.K.8, W.1.8, W.2.8, W.3.8. Recall information from experiences or gather information from provided sources to answer a question.

Range of Writing

- W.3.10. Write routinely over extended time frames (time for research, reflection, and revision) and shorter time frames (a single sitting or a day or two) for a range of discipline-specific tasks, purposes, and audiences.

Speaking & Listening

Comprehension and Collaboration

- SL.K.1, SL.1.1, SL.2.1. Participate in collaborative conversations with diverse partners about grade-level topics and texts with peers and adults in small and larger groups.

- SL.K.2, SL.1.2, SL.2.2, SL.3.2. Recount or describe key ideas or details from a text read aloud or information presented orally or through other media.

- SL.K.3, SL.1.3, SL.2.3, SL.3.3. Ask and answer questions about what a speaker says in order to gather additional information or clarify something that is not understood.

Presentation of Knowledge and Ideas

- SL.K.4, SL.1.4, SL.2.4. Describe people, places, things, and events with relevant details, expressing ideas and feelings clearly.

- SL.K.5, SL.1.5, SL.2.5, SL.3.5. Add drawings or other visual displays to stories or recounts of experiences when appropriate to clarify ideas, thoughts, and feelings.

Language

Conventions of Standard English

- L.K.1, L.1.1, L.2.1, L.3.1. Demonstrate command of the conventions of standard English grammar and usage when writing or speaking.

- L.K.2, L.1.2, L.2.2, L.3.2. Demonstrate command of the conventions of standard English capitalization, punctuation, and spelling when writing.

Knowledge of Language

- L.2.3, L.3.3. Use knowledge of language and its conventions when writing, speaking, reading, or listening.

Vocabulary Acquisition and Use

- L.K.4, L.1.4, L.2.4, L.3.4. Determine or clarify the meaning of unknown and multiple-meaning words and phrases based on grade level reading and content, choosing flexibly from an array of strategies.

- L.K.6, L.1.6, L.2.6, L.3.6. Use words and phrases acquired through conversations, reading and being read to, and responding to texts.

CALENDAR TIME

Getting Started

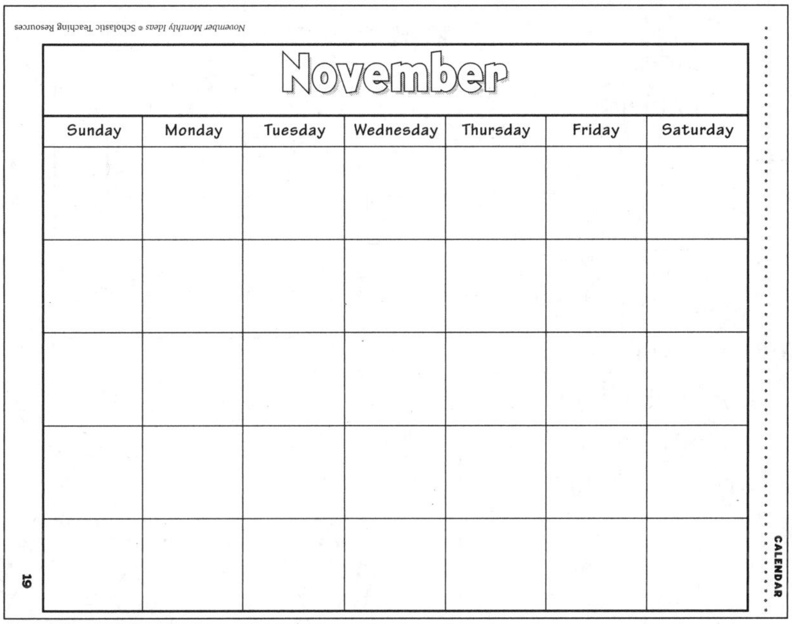
November Monthly Ideas © Scholastic Teaching Resources

November

Sunday	Monday	Tuesday	Wednesday	Thursday	Friday	Saturday

19

CALENDAR

★ MARK YOUR CALENDAR

Make photocopies of the calendar grid on page 19 and use it to meet your needs. Consider using the write-on spaces to:

- Write the corresponding numerals for each day
- Mark and count how many days have passed
- Track the weather with stamps or stickers
- Note student birthdays
- Record homework assignments
- Communicate with families about positive behaviors
- Remind volunteers about scheduling, field trips, shortened days, and so on

CELEBRATIONS THIS MONTH

Whether you post a photocopy of pages 20 through 23 near your class calendar or just turn to these pages for inspiration, you're sure to find lots of information on them to discuss with students. To take celebrating and learning a step further, invite the class to add more to the list. For example, students can add anniversaries of significant events and the birthdays of their favorite authors or historical figures.

 ## CALENDAR HEADER

You can make a photocopy of the header on page 24, color it, and use it as a title for your classroom calendar. You might opt to give the coloring job to a student who has a birthday that month. The student is sure to enjoy seeing his or her artwork each and every day of the month.

 ## BEFORE INTRODUCING WHAT'S THE WEATHER?

Make a photocopy of the body template on page 25. Laminate it so you can use it again and again. Before sharing the template with the class, cut out pieces of cloth in the shapes of clothing students typically wear this month. For example, if you live in a warm weather climate, your November attire might include shorts and t-shirts. If you live in chillier climates, your attire might include a scarf, hat, and coat. Fit the cutouts to the body outline. When the clothing props are made, and you're ready to have students dress the template, display the clothing. Invite the "weather helper of the day" to tell what pieces of clothing he or she would choose to dress appropriately for the weather. (For extra fun, use foam to cut out accessories such as an umbrella, sunhat, and raincoat.)

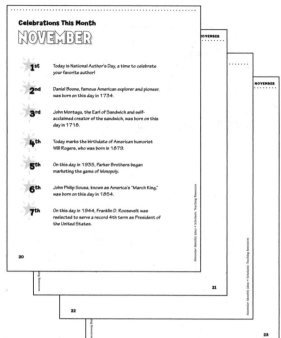

November

Sunday	Monday	Tuesday	Wednesday	Thursday	Friday	Saturday

Celebrations This Month

NOVEMBER

1st Today is National Author's Day, a time to celebrate your favorite author!

2nd Daniel Boone, famous American explorer and pioneer, was born on this day in 1734.

3rd John Montagu, the Earl of Sandwich and self-acclaimed creator of the sandwich, was born on this day in 1718.

4th Today marks the birthdate of American humorist Will Rogers, who was born in 1879.

5th On this day in 1935, Parker Brothers began marketing the game of *Monopoly*.

6th John Philip Sousa, known as America's "March King," was born on this day in 1854.

7th On this day in 1944, Franklin D. Roosevelt was reelected to serve a record 4th term as President of the United States.

8th Edmund Halley, famous English astronomer and the first to predict the return appearance of a comet, was born on this day in 1656.

9th On this day in 1872, a fire destroyed hundreds of buildings and took 14 lives in Boston, prompting a new system of fire prevention laws and regulations.

10th "Sesame Street" made its broadcast debut on this day in 1969.

11th In 1918, at the 11th hour of the 11th day of the 11th month, World War I came to an end. We observe Veteran's Day annually on this day to remember this important event.

12th In 1815, Elizabeth Cady Stanton, a leader of the women's suffrage movement in America, was born on this day.

13th One of the most visited sites in Washington, D.C.—the Vietnam Veterans Memorial—was dedicated on this day in 1982.

14th Robert Fulton, American inventor of the steamboat, was born on this day in 1765.

15th Georgia O'Keefe, an American artist known for her landscape paintings of the Southwest, was born on this day in 1887.

16th The first Harry Potter movie, *Harry Potter and the Sorcerer's Stone* by J. K. Rowling, was released in the United States on this day in 2001.

17th The Suez Canal, which connects the Mediterranean and Red Seas, was opened to shipping on this day in 1869.

18th Today marks the birthdate of Mickey Mouse, who made his first appearance in a sound cartoon in 1928.

19th On this day in 1863, President Abraham Lincoln delivered his 272-word Gettysburg Address at a military cemetery.

20th *Zarya*, the first module of the International Space Station, was launched on this day in 1998.

21st Today is World Hello Day, a day on which world leaders are encouraged to communicate rather than use force to resolve conflicts.

22nd On this day in 1963, U.S. President John F. Kennedy was assassinated while riding in a motorcade in Dallas, Texas.

23rd On this day in 1868, Louis Ducos du Hauron was granted a patent on a process for making color photographs.

24th Father Junipero Serra, founder of the California Missions, was born on this day in 1713.

25th American industrialist and philanthropist Andrew Carnegie was born on this day in 1835.

26th Currently celebrated on the fourth Thursday in November, Thanksgiving Day has been an annual tradition since President Abraham Lincoln declared a national day of "thanksgiving" on this day in 1863.

27th The first Macy's Thanksgiving Day Parade, featuring store employees and animals from the Central Park Zoo, was held in New York City on this day in 1924.

28th American architect Henry Bacon, who designed the Lincoln Memorial in Washington, D.C., was born on this day in 1866.

29th Louisa May Alcott, author of *Little Women*, was born on this day in 1832.

30th American author and humorist Samuel Clemens, better known as Mark Twain, was born on this day in 1835.

ELECTION TIME

Every four years, the American people vote to elect the President of the United States. From the campaign trail to their political party's convention and right up to Election Day, presidential candidates share their vision and promises for the nation, in the hopes of being chosen for the highest office of the land. Then, on the first Tuesday of November in the year of the general election, citizens of voting age—18 years old or older—head to the polls to cast their votes. It is this process that makes the United States a country that is governed by and for the people.

Although many other government officials are elected during the general election, state, county, and local municipalities may schedule and hold elections more frequently or on different dates. The following activities focus on the people, places, and process of a presidential election, but many can be easily adapted for use with state and local elections, or even elections you might hold in your own classroom.

Suggested Activities

 ## WHO'S QUALIFIED?

Review with students the qualifications a candidate must meet to run for President of the United States: the person must be a natural-born citizen of the United States, have been a resident for 14 years, and be at least 35 years old. Explain that there is no maximum age requirement for the office. Then share that the youngest person to be elected president was John F. Kennedy, at the age of 43. The oldest was Ronald Reagan at 69 years old. Challenge students to research the age of the current president on his or her election and then to find out the age of each presidential candidate for the upcoming election.

★ PARTY PICKS

Tell students that the two major political parties in the United States are the Democratic and Republican parties. While there may be candidates on the presidential ballot for a third party, the president is usually elected from one of the two major parties. Ask students to identify the candidates for each party. Have them choose a candidate to research and write about. Distribute copies of the candidate information sheet (page 31) for students to complete. They might also draw a picture to go along with the completed sheet. Then prepare a bulletin board using the symbols and characters that represent each party. (If desired, enlarge the characters on pages 32–33.) Display students' work with the appropriate character.

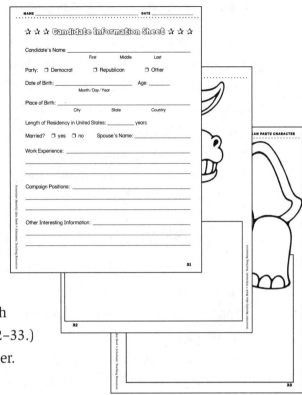

★ WHAT ARE THE ISSUES?

Work with students to list some of the major issues of the presidential campaign. Ask them to share what they know about each candidate's views on these issues. If desired, invite them to bring in campaign literature, mailers, newspaper ads, political cartoons, and so on to share and discuss. After reviewing, create a table display for each political party. Purchase or make a tri-fold project board and cover it with gift wrap in patriotic colors or paper in the color represented with that party (typically, blue for the Democratic party and red for the Republican party). Stand each board on a table and display campaign literature and memorabilia for each party on the corresponding board. Invite students to add the stand-up party characters (page 34) to the displays. To prepare, copy the patterns onto tagboard. Have students choose a character to color and cut out. (They might use red, white, and blue, adding stars and stripes to embellish their animals.) Then ask them to write about a candidate or a position about a campaign issue on the back of the cut out. After sharing their work with the class, have students fold their cutout and stand it upright near the board for that political party.

★ PLATFORMS AND PROMISES

Presidential candidates run for office by stating their platforms—the political policy and views they hold—and making promises to the voters. Talk about the basic platform of each political party in the election and discuss some of the promises made by the candidates. Then invite students to make one of the following projects, choosing a candidate to feature in the project. In either project, students will include their candidate's platform and promises.

Campaign Mobile

Cut out a copy of the mobile topper (page 35) and star patterns (page 36). Write the candidate's name on the topper. Then write a different promise made by the candidate on each star. Or, write about that candidate's policies or views. If desired, color the parts of the mobile, adding a patriotic border around the edges of the stars. Use tape and yarn to hang stars from the topper, then add a yarn hanger to the mobile.

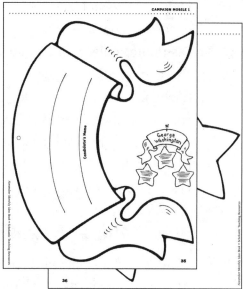

Stand-Up Paper-Bag Eagle

To prepare for this project, students will need a copy of the eagle head and two wings (page 37), a paper bag, and construction paper. Have them follow the directions below to make their paper-bag eagle. Stand the projects on the edge of a table or bookshelf to display.

1. Cut out the eagle head and wings. Glue the patterns to a paper bag. (The head should be at the open end of the bag.)

2. Write the candidate's promises and/or platform on the wings and front of the bag.

3. Open the bag and fill it with crumpled paper. Then fold down the top and glue it in place.

4. Cut construction-paper tail feathers and glue to the back of the bag at the bottom.

★ CAMPAIGN BUTTON

Invite students to put themselves in the place of a candidate running for office, whether for president, vice-president, state governor, city mayor, county commissioner, or any other elected office. What would they expect to accomplish if voted into that position? What campaign promises would they make? What changes would they make to help improve the lives or situations of voters? Discuss student responses. Then distribute copies of the giant campaign button (page 38) for students to complete and sign. If desired, they can put a piece of double-sided tape on the back of their button and wear it on their shirt. As an alternative, invite students to make buttons to use for their own campaign, if running for a school or class office.

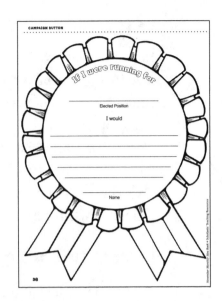

★ THE CAMPAIGN IS ON!

Create a display to highlight students' campaign buttons (above). First cover the display board with red, white, and blue gift wrap, or attach strips of white paper over a red or blue background to make a striped background. Enlarge the eagle head and wing patterns (page 37) to use as a display topper. (Add construction-paper tail feathers, if desired.) Then attach the campaign buttons to the display.

★ PATRIOTIC CAMPAIGNER

Let students make and wear these props to tout the campaign promises and positions they stated on their campaign buttons (above)—or to express those of their favorite candidate. First, distribute copies of the Uncle Sam hat and beard patterns (pages 39–40) for students to color and cut out. Have them staple the hat to a 2- by 24-inch strip of construction paper, and then fit the strip to their head, stapling the ends together and trimming the excess. Invite students to don their hat and beard as they campaign for their imaginary office, or for an actual candidate in a public or class election.

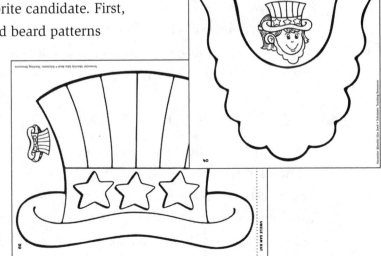

LET'S VOTE!

Hold a mock election in class to let students pick their preferred presidential candidate. Fill in the candidates' names on a copy of the appropriate ballot (page 41). Then copy and cut out a supply of the ballots. On Election Day, ask children to mark their ballots and put them into a paper bag. Afterward, tally and compare the class election results with students. (For class elections, you might use the other ballot provided on page 41.)

 ## VOTER FUN GLASSES

After students submit their presidential votes for the class tally, invite them to make and wear a pair of glasses to celebrate their participation in the election process. Distribute copies of the glasses patterns on page 42. Have students color and cut out the patterns, carefully cutting the slits on the glasses frame and the earpieces. To assemble, students simply fit each earpiece into the corresponding slit on the frame. If desired, students can take their glasses home to give to a voting family member on Election Day.

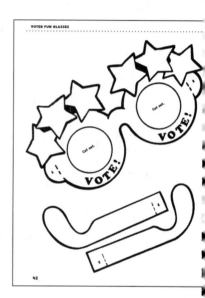

 ## REAL RESULTS

Encourage students to watch television coverage of the presidential election results. Encourage them to record the total votes from each state as they are reported. At school the next day, display a large map of the United States. Invite students to attach a removable red or blue sticker dot to each state to indicate which presidential candidate won that state's vote. (You might explain that at least 270 votes by the electoral college are needed to win the election.) Compare the vote results, then tell students that the newly elected president will take office in a special swearing-in ceremony on Inauguration Day the following January.

ELECTION WORD FIND

Wrap up your studies with a word puzzle (page 43) that invites students to find words associated with a presidential election. To take vocabulary-building one step further, record the terms from the word find on a word wall. Then invite students to visit the word wall for inspiration in election-related writing assignments.

NAME ______________________________ DATE ______________

☆ ☆ ☆ Candidate Information Sheet ☆ ☆ ☆

Candidate's Name ____
First Middle Last

Party: ❐ Democrat ❐ Republican ❐ Other

Date of Birth: ______________________________ Age: ________
Month / Day / Year

Place of Birth: ____
City State Country

Length of Residency in United States: __________ years

Married? ❐ yes ❐ no Spouse's Name: ______________________

Work Experience: ____

____

____

Campaign Positions: ____

____

____

Other Interesting Information: __________________________________

____

____

PLACE THIS SIDE ALONG FOLD.

PLACE THIS SIDE ALONG FOLD.

34

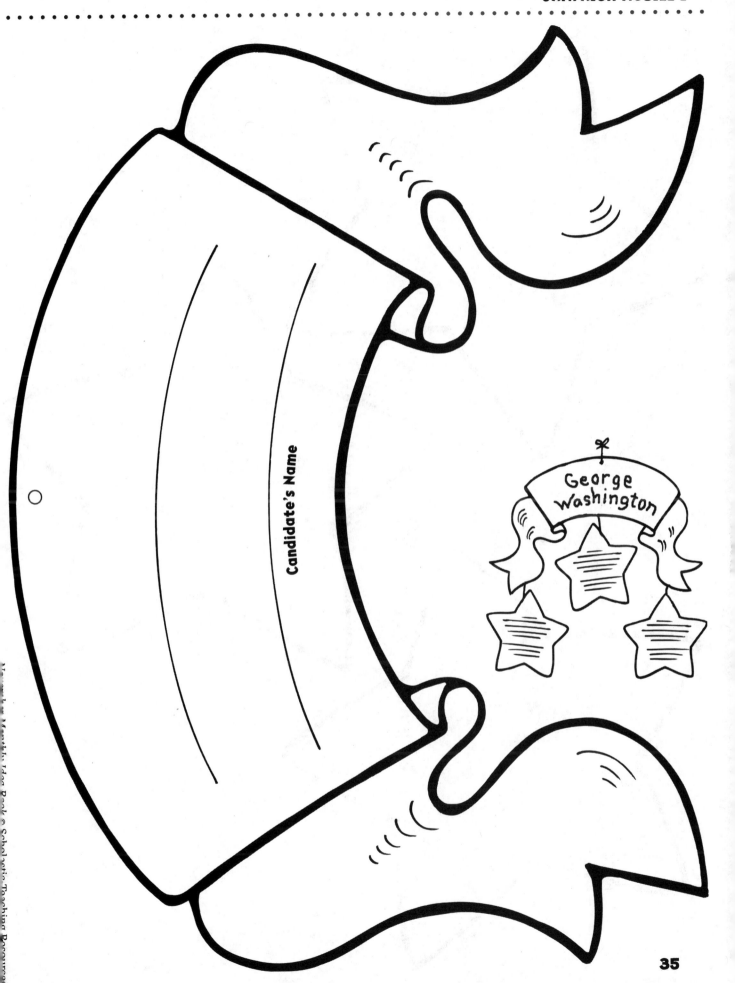

Candidate's Name

George Washington

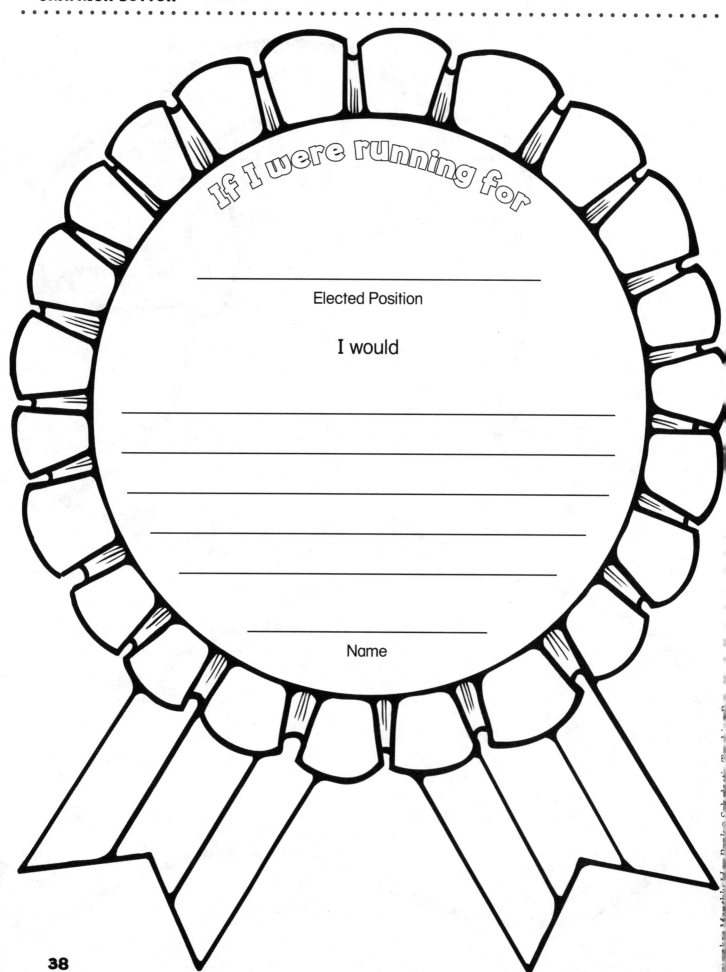

If I were running for

Elected Position

I would

Name

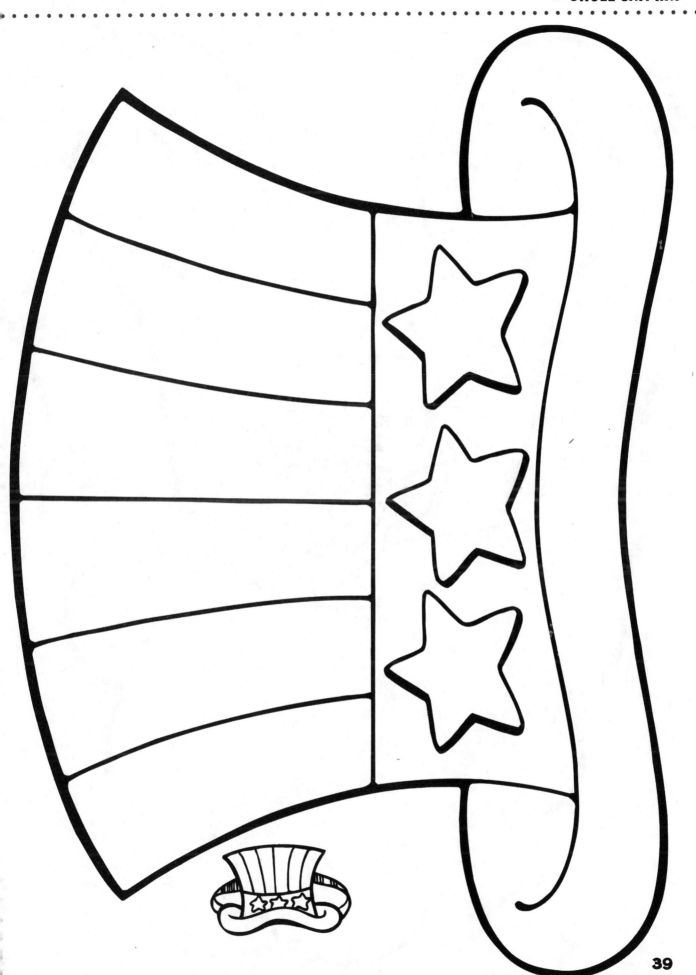

41

Class Election Ballot

POSITION

☐ _____ Candidate

☐ _____ Candidate

☐ _____ Candidate

POSITION

☐ _____ Candidate

☐ _____ Candidate

☐ _____ Candidate

General Election Ballot

DEMOCRATIC PARTY

☐ _____ President

_____ Vice President

REPUBLICAN PARTY

☐ _____ President

_____ Vice President

OTHER PARTY

☐ _____ President

_____ Vice President

Election Word Find

Find these words in the puzzle below:

BALLOT   CAMPAIGN   CANDIDATE   CONVENTION   DEMOCRAT
ELECTION   INAUGURATION   NATION   NOVEMBER   PRESIDENT
REPUBLICAN   SPEECH   TERM   VICE PRESIDENT   VOTE

```
S V R T G H Y K L H N S P E E C H F B N K L Y
X Z A S W Q R T H Y B H R D C V T Y H U J M H
D C X V C A N D I D A T E F H J I I L K M N G
V F G H O S X V B H L J S F T Y N A T I O N P
W R T Y N C H Y U I L N I B G H A R Y U I O P
C V G Y V H U I K J O R D S W E U C V C W Q E
Q S X D E G B F D R T U E D S W G F R A F V B
M L K O N O V E M B E R N O K J U J K M F G T
E L E C T I O N D R T Y T H N J R H G P C V B
R T Y U I S R T G H U J K I O L A G H A C X Z
L P O I O G F D E M O C R A T F T A W I D R T
S G H U N G H Y U I K M N H U Y I F T G E W Y
V I C E P R E S I D E N T F G T O F N N C E T
O F R H G B N M K I L O H B G Y N R F D E W S
T E R M C D F R E P U B L I C A N F R H Y U K
E S C V T G B N J U I K M K L O P M N J H Y T
X D R T G V B H U J M N H Y T R E W Q A S D E
F R G B N J I U H J K L O P M N B V G F R Q W
```

Use eight or more words from the puzzle to write a paragraph about
the importance of voting. Use the back of this page.

STATES & CAPITALS

Since 1776, the United States of America has grown from 13 colonies to 50 states. Each state in our nation has its own unique history and characteristics. With the activities in this unit, students learn about the background, geography, people, natural resources, and historical facts about the state they live in. In addition, they can complete activities that help them learn all of the state names, locations, and capitals.

Suggested Activities

★ ALL ABOUT MY STATE

Start your study on states by having students complete a book report about their own state. First, help them locate their state on a large map of the United States. Talk about which region of the country the state belongs to and point out notable geographic characteristics of the state. Then have students conduct research to learn facts about the state, such as its capital, population, resources, and other interesting and historical information. Copy and distribute pages 47–53 for students to complete with their findings. When finished, have students sequence and stack the pages behind the cover and then staple them together along the left side.

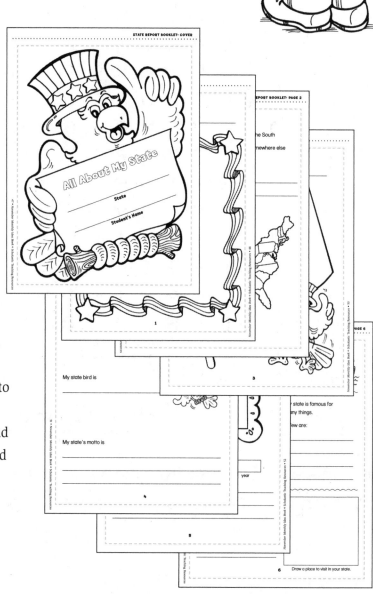

★ STATE-SHAPED BOOKS

Invite students to choose a state to research and write about. They can include information about the state's geography, history, people, and so on in their writing. In addition, they might include stories about real or imaginary visits to interesting sites in their state. To create a book cover, ask students to fold a large sheet of construction paper in half and draw an outline of their state on the page, filling the page with the shape and using the fold as one of the state borders. Have them cut out the shape through both thicknesses, leaving the fold intact. Then have students cut out the same shape from plain sheets of paper, write their findings on the pages, then bind their pages inside the state-shaped cover.

★ NAME THAT STATE!

Give children practice in recognizing the 50 states by their shape on a map. Distribute copies of the map on page 54. Then have students number a sheet of paper from 1 to 50. Ask them to write the name of each state by its number. When finished, students can refer to a large map of the United States to check their answers. (Or, use the answers on page 143.)

★ STATE LOCATORS

For a fun variation of Name That State! (above), give clues to help students identify specific states. For example, "Alabama borders the Gulf of Mexico. Color that state green." Or "California is on the Pacific Coast. Color it yellow." Or "Nevada is to the east of California. Put an X on it."

★ STATE NAMES

Invite students to research the origin of each state name. Explain that states derived their names from many different sources. Some, like South Dakota and Illinois, were named for Native American tribes or territories. Others were named for early leaders, such as Pennsylvania for William Penn. Have students write their findings on large index cards, then post the cards near each state on a large map of the United States. For interior states, they can use yarn to connect the card to the state. To expand the activity, challenge students to research each state's nickname to add to the display.

★ WHAT IS THE CAPITAL?

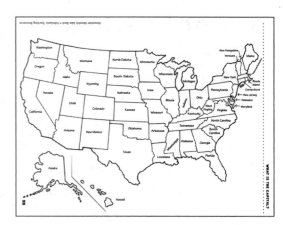

Distribute copies of the map on page 55. Ask students to write each state name on a sheet of paper and then write that state's capital next to its name. (If desired, list all of the state capitals on a sheet of chart paper for students to use as a reference.) When finished, have them use a large map of the United States to check their answers. (Or, use the answers on page 143.) How many states and capitals did they match correctly?

★ STATE CAPITAL CONTEST

Divide your class into several teams. Then choose a contestant from a team and name a state. Ask that contestant to tell the name of that state's capital. If he or she is unable to provide the correct response, give a contestant on another team the opportunity to respond. Continue, passing from one team to the next, until a contestant names the correct capital and earns a point for the team. Keep playing until the teams have identified the capitals of all 50 states. For a variation, name a capital and have contestants identify the corresponding state.

★ STATES AND CAPITALS BINGO

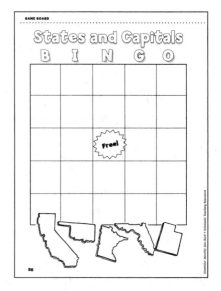

Use this fun game to give students practice in learning the states and capitals. First, distribute copies of the Bingo game board (page 56). Have students write a different state name in each box. Then give them a handful of markers. To make caller cards, write the name of each state's capital on a separate index card and place in a paper bag. (You might write the state name in small print at the bottom of each card.) To play, draw a card from the bag and read the name of the capital aloud. If students have the corresponding state on their game board, they cover that space with a marker. The first student to cover five spaces in a row calls out "Bingo!" Check the covered boxes on that student's game board against the called cards to make sure they all match. If so, the student wins the game. For a variation, have students write the state capitals on their game boards, then label the caller cards with the state names.

All About My State

State

Student's Name

My state's capital is _____

Here is a drawing of my state.

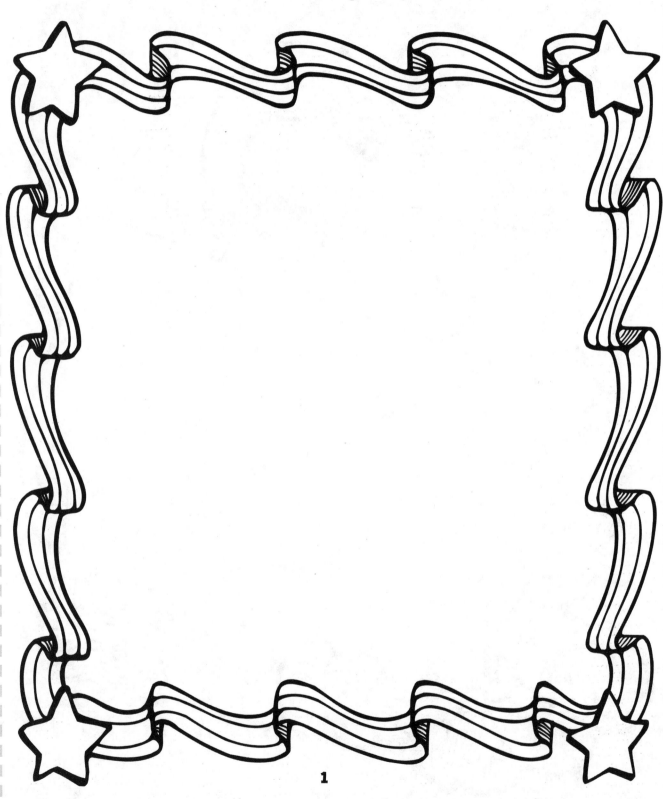

November Monthly Idea Book ©Scholastic Teaching Resources • 48

My state is located:

☐ in the West   ☐ in the Midwest   ☐ in the South

☐ in the Northeast   ☐ in the Southwest   ☐ somewhere else

My state is colored _____.

                          Color

My state is bordered by _____

_____

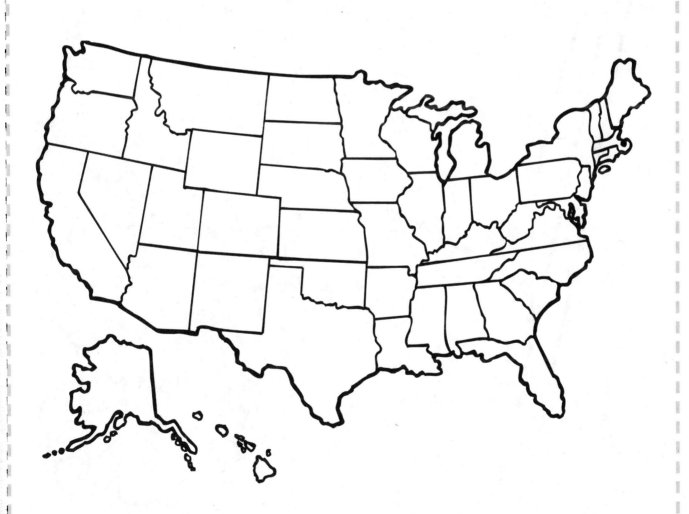

This is my state's flag.

The flag's main colors are _____

My state's nickname is _____

My state was admitted to the Union in _____
Year

My state flower is

_____

My state bird is

_____

My state's motto is

_____

_____

_____

My state has a population of about _____ people.

A famous person from my state is _____

Draw the person's picture.

This person was born in [   ] and died in [   ] .
                             year   year

This person is famous for _____

_____

_____

Some important main rivers, lakes, and mountains are

_____

_____

My state has many
natural resources.

A few are:

1. _____

2. _____

3. _____

4. _____

My state is famous for
many things.

A few are:

1. _____

2. _____

3. _____

4. _____

One reason to visit my state is

_____

_____

_____

Draw a place to visit in your state.

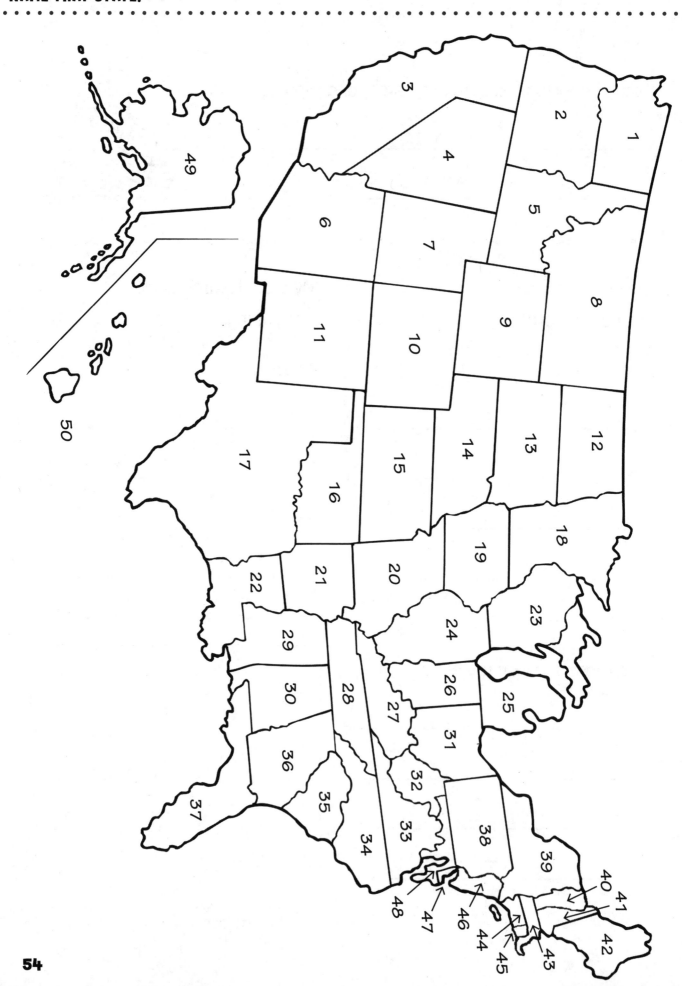

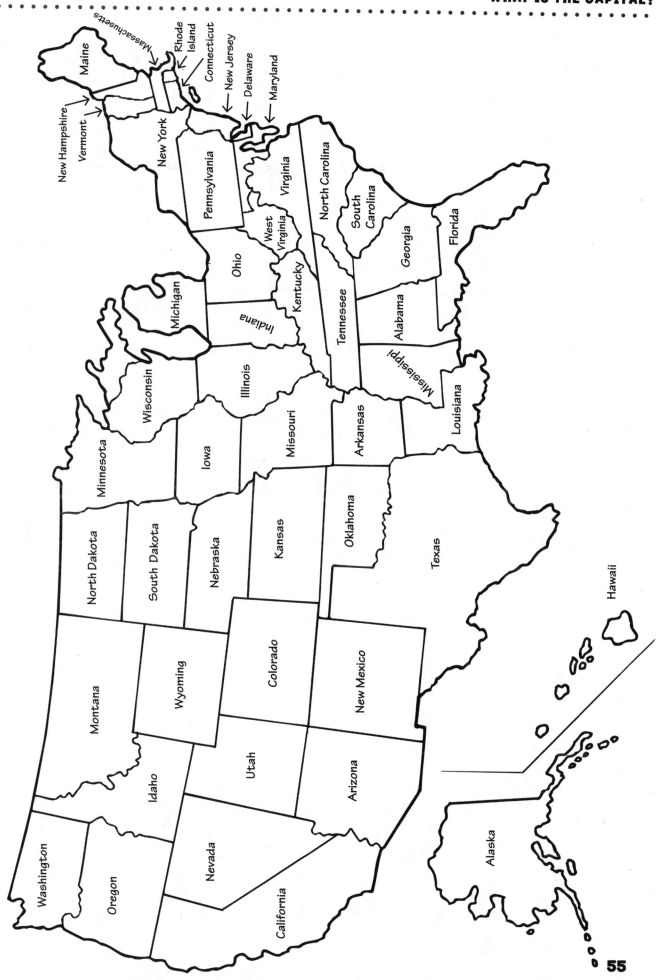

States and Capitals
B I N G O

		Free!		

WOODLAND ANIMALS

Woodlands—or forests—are habitats where trees are the reigning plant form, although a great number of other plants also grow in this environment. Woodland plants, such as trees, shrubs, grasses, mosses, ferns, and flowering herbs offer a wide range of shelter and food choices for animals. The type of animals that inhabit a particular forest depends largely on the available vegetation and each animal's diet and other needs. Some common woodland animals include squirrels, owls, bears, raccoons, rabbits, mice, skunks, lizards, and frogs. While some animals live in the woods all of the time, others spend only a part of their time there. In fact, some woodland animals can be found in rural areas, as well as in and around most cities.

Suggested Activities

★ MY ANIMAL REPORT

Many kinds of animals live in the woods—mammals, birds, reptiles, and amphibians. Work with students to make a list of woodland animals including squirrels, owls, raccoons, and bears. You might also list rabbits, fox, mice, skunks, and bats. Then have students do research on a woodland animal that they choose from the list. (Or, assign an animal to each student.) Students can use books available in the classroom as well as library books, Internet resources, and other sources such as videos and personal interviews for their research. Distribute photocopies of page 61 for students to complete using their findings. Finally, have them write a story about their animal on the back of the page. Encourage students to share their reports with the class.

★ FLAPPING OWL

Owls are known for their large eyes and nocturnal habits. Invite students to make this owl with movable wings on which to write what they know about owls. They might record owl facts on the body (and wings), or write poems, rhymes, or stories about this fascinating bird. To assemble,

(continued)

have students cut out photocopies of the owl patterns (pages 62–63), then use brass fasteners to attach the wings to their owl body. If desired, copy the owl patterns onto light brown construction paper, or invite students to color their completed owls. To "flap" the owl's wings, students simply move the wings to the sides away from the owl's body then back to the center.

 ## RASCALLY RODENTS

Tell students that squirrels belong to the same family of gnawing animals as chipmunks, mice, beavers, gophers, and porcupines. All of these animals are rodents and often reside in a woodland habitat. Rodents are mammals—they have fur, are warm-blooded, and feed their babies milk from their own bodies. They are the only mammals, other than humans, that store their food for the winter. Invite students to choose a rodent to research and write about. Afterward, collect their written work and bind the pages to a photocopy of the book cover on page 64. Add a title and author line, invite a volunteer to color the cover, then place the book in your class library for students to enjoy.

 ## RESEARCHING RACCOONS

Ask students to do research to learn and write about the remarkable raccoon! You might provide a list of questions such as the following to help guide their research:

- What do raccoons eat?
- Where do they live?
- How do they take care of their young?
- When are raccoons most active?
- Can raccoons climb or swim?
- Are raccoons hibernators?

When finished, distribute photocopies of the patterns (page 65) to students and invite them to make raccoon page framers on which to display their reports. To assemble, students simply color and cut out their patterns, glue the raccoon head to the top of a sheet of black construction paper and the tail to the bottom, then attach their written work to the "body."

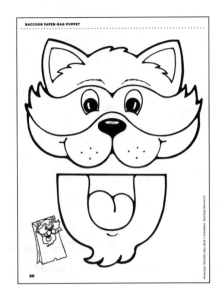

★ RACCOON PAPER-BAG PUPPET

Invite students to make raccoon puppets to use for role-playing and dramatizations about woodland animals, or to use as props for presentations. To begin, distribute small paper bags and photocopies of the raccoon patterns (page 66) to students. Have them color and cut out the patterns, then glue their raccoon's head to the bottom flap of a bag and its mouth to the front of the bag below the flap.

★ WOODLAND ANIMAL PROJECTS

Encourage students to learn about different woodland animals (or learn more about those they are already familiar with). Then invite them to share their findings with partners, small groups, or the whole class. Following are some projects they might make (depending on their animal choice) to use as props for their presentations.

Animal Masks

Provide a choice of the mask patterns on pages 67–69 (copied onto tagboard), along with an assortment of craft materials for students to use in decorating their masks. Have students cut out their mask and the eyeholes. After decorating, help them punch a hole in and attach a yarn tie to each side of their mask.

Stand-Up Squirrel

Photocopy a supply of the squirrel and acorn patterns (page 70) onto construction paper. (You might use light brown, red, or gray paper for the squirrel.) Distribute the patterns and glue (or tape) to students. Then have them do the following to make a stand-up squirrel:

1. Cut out the patterns.

2. Fold the squirrel's legs toward the center of its body.

3. Glue the acorn between the squirrel's paws.

4. Fold the squirrel's tail back along the dashed line, as shown.

5. Stand the squirrel on a flat surface, such as a table or windowsill.

59

ANIMALS-OF-THE-WOODS PICTURE PROPS

Use the patterns on page 71 in a variety of ways to help enhance and reinforce students' learning about woodland animals. For example, you can enlarge the patterns for use on bulletin board displays. Or have students do research to find facts about each animal. Ask them to write their facts on note cards (one fact per card), then post the cards next to the corresponding animals. Alternately, you might laminate the animal cutouts and attach a hook-and-loop fastener to the back of each one. Then invite students to use the figures on a flannelboard to share facts or tell stories about the animals.

 ## PEEK-IN TREES

Make a peek-in tree for each kind of woodland animal that students have been learning about. Simply color and cut out photocopies of the tree on page 72. Then cut along the bold line on each tree trunk to create a flap that opens and closes. Glue each tree to a sheet of construction paper and attach a picture of an animal behind the trunk flap. (You might use the animals on page 71, as well as magazine cutouts or animals from coloring books.) Then display the trees on a bulletin board and surround each one with clue cards about the animal hiding in the trunk. Students can read the clues, guess the animal, and open the flap and peek in to check their answer. If desired, invite students to make their own peek-in trees to take home.

 ## "NUTTY" ABOUT LEARNING!

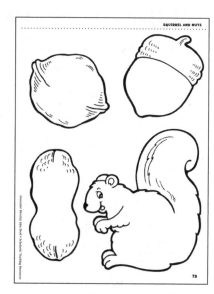

Photocopy, color, and cut out a supply of the squirrel and nut patterns (page 73) to use for a variety of activities. For example, you might write addition facts on the nuts and sums on the squirrels to create a matching activity. Or, label the cutouts with sight words or vocabulary words for students to use as flash cards. You might also have students do patterning activities with the nuts. If desired, use an overhead projector to trace large images of the items onto poster board or bulletin board paper. Then cut out and use the images to create displays or signs to post around the room.

NAME ______________________________ DATE ______________

My Animal Report

My animal is

____

Animal name

My animal lives in

____

____

It eats ______________________________

____

____

[ ]

This is a picture of my animal.

My animal can grow to about this size: ______________________________

Here are some special things about my animal: ______________________________

____

____

____

In the winter, my animal ______________________________

____

My animal is: ❒ endangered ❒ not endangered

What might happen if you met this animal in the wild? Use the back of this page to write about your imaginary experience.

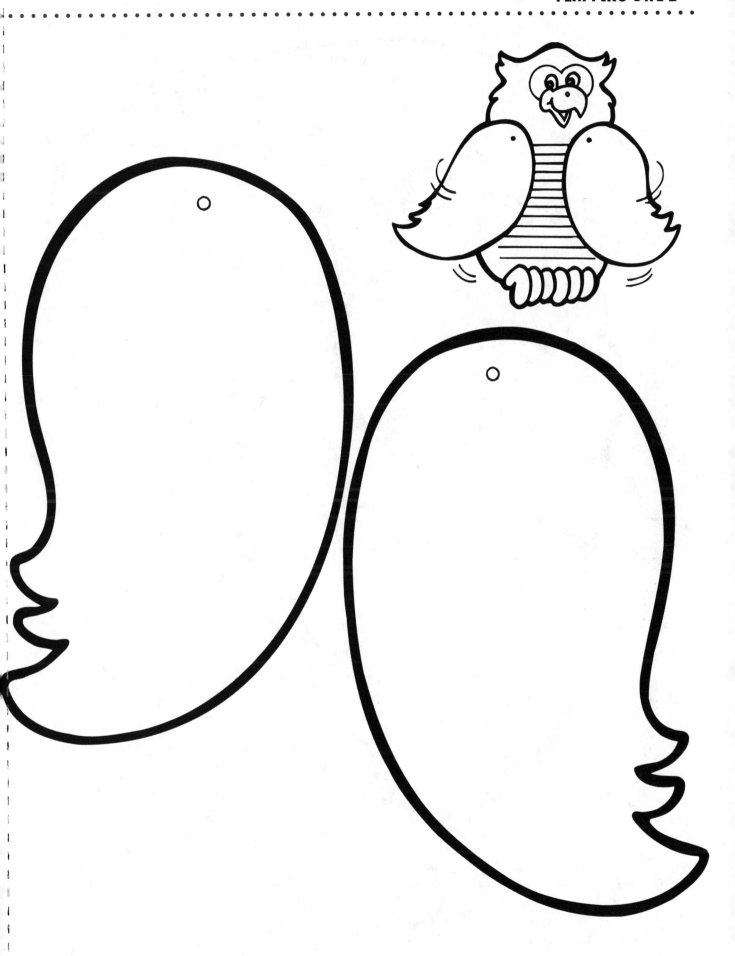

PLACE THIS SIDE ALONG FOLD.

64

November Monthly Idea Book © Scholastic Teaching Resources

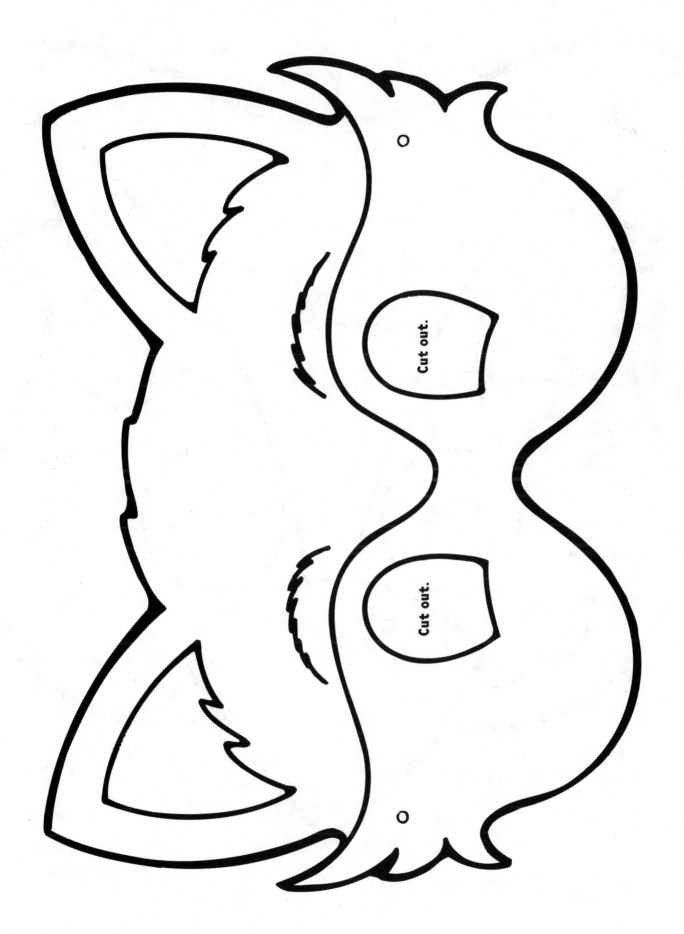

Cut out.

Cut out.

Cut out.

Cut out.

Cut out.

Cut out.

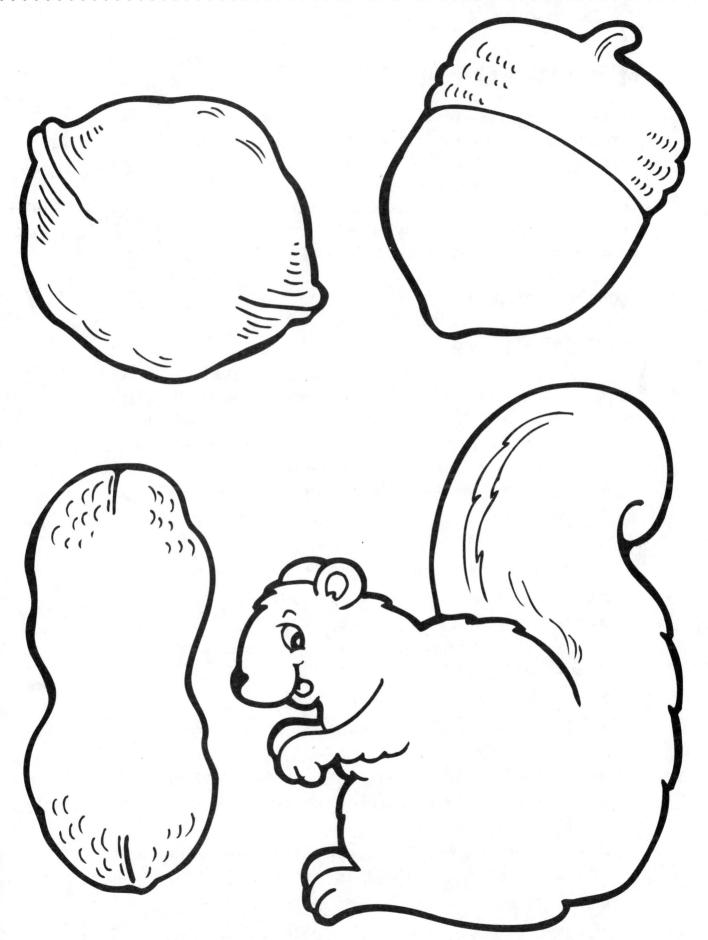

REV UP FOR READING!

Children's Book Week, a national literacy initiative formerly observed during the third week in November, was moved to the month of May in 2008. Although the date of this important celebration has been changed, reading throughout the year is important and beneficial to students at all levels. The activities in this unit give students a head start on reading a variety of books and help build their enthusiasm for reading in the months leading up to Children's Book Week.

Suggested Activities

 ## READ AND RESPOND

Provide a variety of books, both fiction and nonfiction, from which students can choose to read. Place the books in your class library, or work with the media specialist to set up an area in the school library for your class. Rotate the books on a regular basis to give students a wide range of book choices throughout the year. Also encourage them to select and read books from home or the public library. Then instruct students to do some of the following to respond to and/or report on their reading activities:

- Choose two characters from a story and write a conversation they might have about an event in the book.

- Write a letter to a close friend to recommend a book you have just read.

- Make a list of new, unusual, or interesting words or phrases in a book.

- Write a television commercial to try to "sell" a book you have read. Recruit classmates to help you prepare for and practice the commercial before acting it out for the class.

- Draw a cartoon strip using characters from a book.

- Write a different ending to a story you have read. Add illustrations, if desired. Then share your new ending with classmates.

- Write a letter to the author of your book, telling him or her why you did (or did not) like the story. Or, write a suggestion for a sequel or new characters that might be added to the story.

- Design a poster or book jacket for your book. Obtain permission to display your project in the classroom or school library.

- Draw a mural depicting events and scenes from a book.

SHARE IT!

Sharing about what they have read is an effective way to help students reflect on a story and demonstrate comprehension. Throughout the school year, invite students to use the following activities to share their reading experiences.

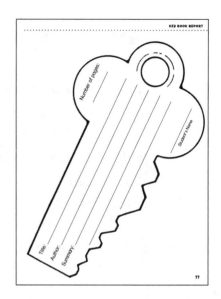

Reading Keys

Photocopy a supply of the Key Book Report on page 77 and place the pages in a basket in your reading center. Invite students to take a page, cut out the key pattern, and fill out the front. If they need more space to write, they can use the back of their key. Display students' keys on a bulletin board titled "Our Keys to Reading!" Or, cut out the keyholes, bind the keys together with a large metal ring, and place them in your class library. When making their reading choices, students can refer to the keys to learn about books that might interest them.

Footprint Reports

Keep photocopies of page 78 available in your literacy center. Then, when students want to share about a book they have read, invite them to cut out a footprint pattern and complete the front. To make a matching pair of footprints, students can cut out another pattern and flip it over to write more about their book on the back. (They might prefer to write an endorsement for their book, or draw pictures depicting characters, scenes, or events from the book.) To display, attach the footprints to the walls to create a winding path that leads to your class library. Add to the display as students continue to read and complete additional footprint reports.

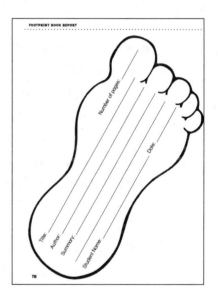

My Book Report

Have students complete the form on page 79 to tell about books they have read. In their summary, encourage students to include information about main characters, settings, key events, and the climax and resolution of the story. (They can use the back of the page if they need more space to write.) Collect students' reports and bind them into a book to put in your class library.

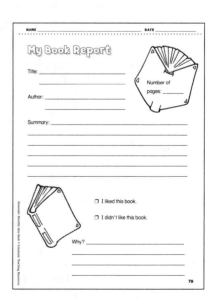

★ PARENT LETTER AND READING RECORD

To encourage parental support for students' reading activities, photocopy the letter and record sheet (pages 80 and 81) and send home a copy of each. Ask students to return the pledge at the bottom of the letter. Then, when they bring in a completed reading record, invite students to share their reading experiences with the class. Attach the returned forms with students' pledges and send new forms home to replace the returned ones. If desired, reward students with a small prize, snack, or privilege each time they complete and return a reading record to class.

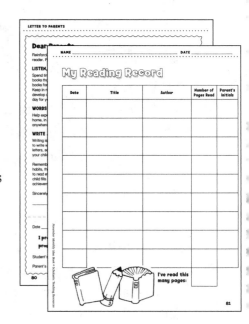

★ MR. BOOKWORM

Use the bookish Mr. Bookworm to guide students to class or library books they might enjoy reading. To prepare, photocopy a supply of page 82. On each page, write a clue that students can use to try to identify or locate a mystery book. When writing the clue, use text that refers specifically to the selected book. You might write the clues from Mr. Bookworm's perspective. For example, for *James and the Giant Peach* by Roald Dahl, your clue might be "I love to go to a peachy-keen place where I spend time with a real 'Dahl'!" After writing the clues, make an additional copy of each one. Place one copy inside the front cover of its corresponding book and the other copy in a basket. Then invite students to choose and read a clue from the basket, guess the mystery book, and find that book in your class or school library. Students can check for the matching clue inside the front cover of the book to see if they found the correct book.

★ CORNER BOOKMARKS

Students can make these bookmarks to use as page placeholders. Distribute tape and photocopies of pages 83 and 84. Ask students to choose a pattern and do the following:

1. Color and cut out the pattern.

2. Fold back the two sides of the cutout where indicated, bringing the straight edges together at the back of the bookmark. Use tape to secure.

3. Slip the bookmark over the top corner of a book to mark the last page read or pages of interest.

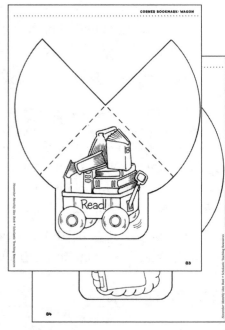

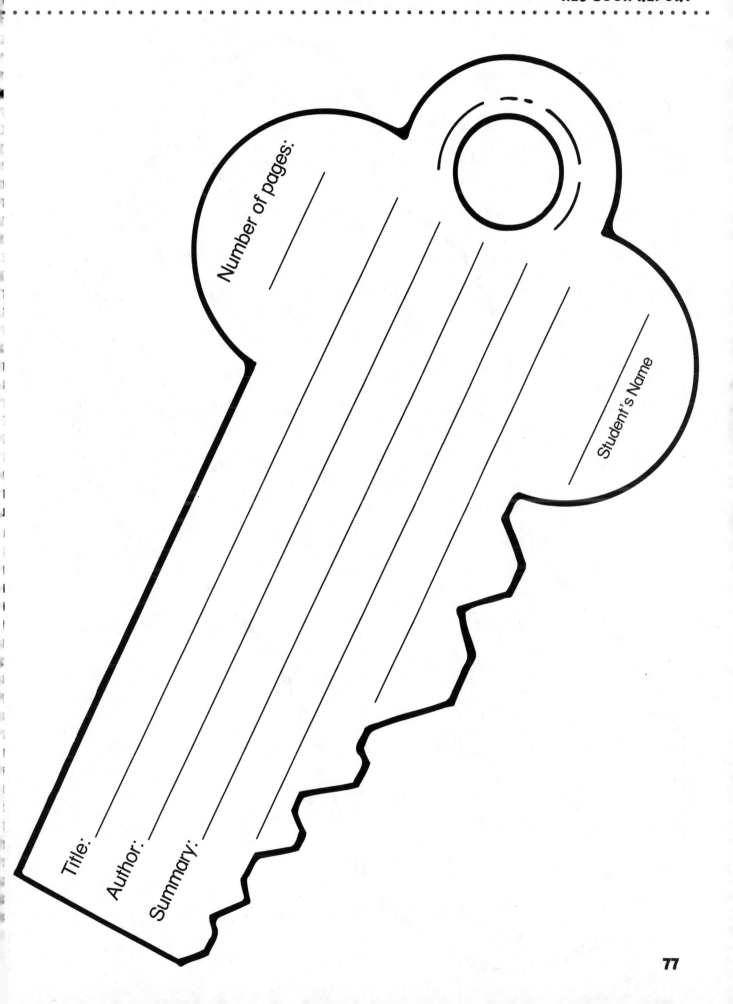

Number of pages: _____

Student's Name _____

Title: _____
Author: _____
Summary: _____

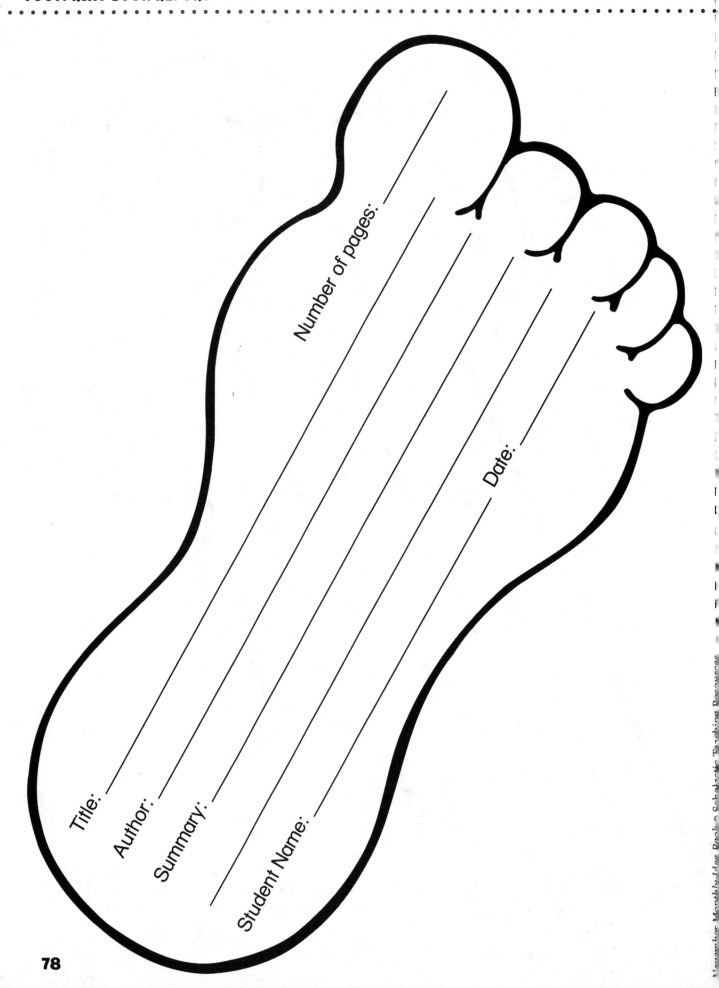

Number of pages: _____

Date: _____

Title: _____

Author: _____

Summary: _____

Student Name: _____

My Book Report

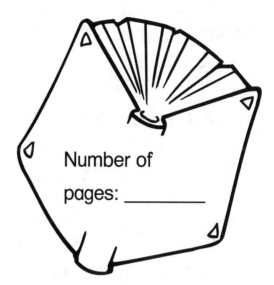

Title: _____

_____

Number of
pages: _____

Author: _____

_____

Summary: _____

_____

_____

_____

_____

_____

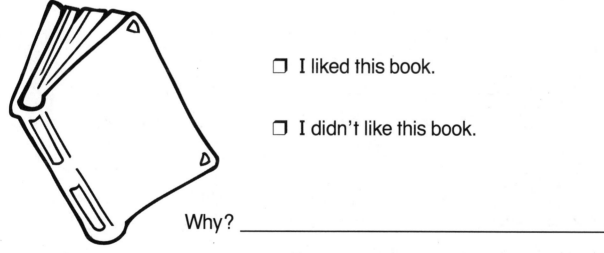

❐ I liked this book.

❐ I didn't like this book.

Why? _____

_____

_____

Dear Parents,

Reinforcing and nurturing reading at home is a great way to help your child become a successful reader. Following are some ways you can help encourage your child to read at home:

LISTEN, TALK, AND READ

Spend time listening to and talking with your child. Quality conversation can lead to sharing about books that your child has read or would like to read. Consider your child's interest when choosing books for him or her. Or, take your child to the library (or book store) to pick out books together. Keep in mind that the more a child reads, or is read to, the more opportunities he or she has to develop and build important literacy skills and good reading habits. Try to set aside quiet time each day for your child to read alone, or with you.

WORDS ARE EVERYWHERE

Help expand your child's awareness of print by pointing out and reading text on food containers at home, in ads or shows that appear on TV, on street and store signs around the community, or most anywhere words appear in your surroundings.

WRITE AND READ

Writing is a good way to help a child learn to read. As children form letters, they eventually learn to write words. This, in turn, provides opportunities for them to explore the relationship between letters, sounds, and words. Keep paper and writing tools (crayons, pencils, and chalk) on hand for your child to use to practice writing letters, words, sentences, and more.

Remember, the more we can work together to help your child develop strong reading skills and habits, the more likely he or she will become a successful reader. Please encourage your child to read every day and keep track of his or her reading on the attached record sheet. After your child fills in the reading record page, please send it to school so your child can share his or her achievement with the class.

Sincerely,

_____

Please cut out the form below, complete it with your child, and return to school.

Date _____

I promise to read _____ pages each day. I will record my progress on my reading record.

Student's Signature _____

Parent's Signature _____

My Reading Record

Date	Title	Author	Number of Pages Read	Parent's Initials

I've read this many pages:

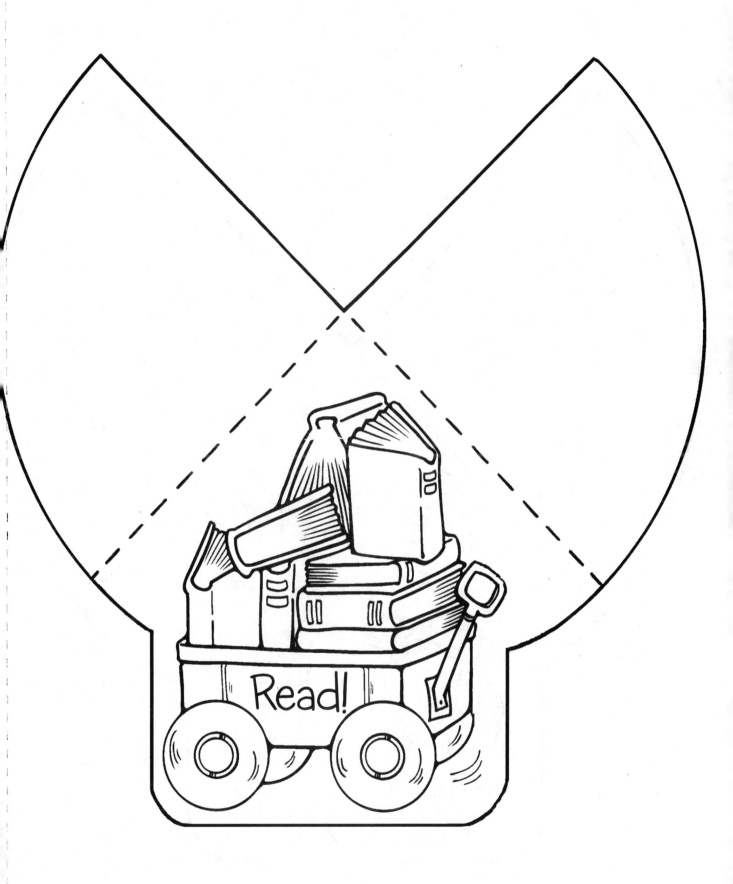

Read!

THANKSGIVING: HISTORY AND HARVEST

On September 6, 1620, a ship named *Mayflower* set sail with 102 people aboard. Many of the passengers, called Pilgrims, left England for a new land where they could practice their religion without being persecuted. After a difficult voyage, the ship reached the shores of North America on November 21, 1620. When they dropped anchor in Plymouth, Massachusetts, the men drew up and signed a document known as the "Mayflower Compact," in which they agreed to remain loyal to the king of England but would establish laws to provide for their own general good and welfare as they settled in the new land.

The first winter in the Pilgrim's new settlement was extremely difficult. Food was scarce and their simple shelters provided little relief from the cold. Many of the Pilgrims died. Fortunately, the Pilgrims found friendship in the native Wampanoags, who taught them how to hunt for food and build sturdier homes. A native called Squanto was instrumental in helping them plant their crops in the spring. By the fall, the Pilgrims had grown and harvested an abundance of food—enough for the present time and to store for the winter. The Pilgrims were so thankful that they held a feast of thanksgiving with their Wampanoag friends.

In the custom of the Pilgrim's first day of thanksgiving in America, our country celebrates Thanksgiving Day on the fourth Thursday of November every year. On that day, family and friends gather to feast, enjoy time together, and give thanks for their many blessings.

Suggested Activities

★ THE *MAYFLOWER*

Invite students to do research to learn and write about the Mayflower. Help them choose a topic, such as facts about the ship, the Pilgrims' route across the sea, or life on the ship. Students might use nonfiction books from the library, the Internet (such as www.plimoth.org), videos, documentaries, and personal interviews as sources for their research. After students complete their reports, distribute photocopies of page 92 and have students make a cover for their written work.

THE MAYFLOWER BOOK COVER

PLACE THIS SIDE ALONG FOLD.

Mayflower

92

★ ACROSS THE OCEAN

Tell students that the Pilgrims had a difficult voyage to America. Living quarters on the ship were crowded and, when they weren't too seasick to eat, the Pilgrims' food choices were mainly limited to salted meat and dry biscuits. Many became sick due to the unclean conditions of the ship. Discuss additional information that students have learned about the voyage of the *Mayflower* and its passengers. Then work with students to label sentence strips (or large index cards) with facts and events about the Pilgrims' trip. Trim each strip close to the text, then use the strips to create a *Mayflower*-related display. To create a ship, enlarge the patterns on page 93 onto poster board. (You might make a few flags.) Color and cut out the patterns and attach to a bulletin board, using long, brown strips of construction paper for masts and flagpoles. For the larger sails, use large rectangles cut from white bulletin board paper or lightweight fabric. After assembling the ship, attach the text strips around it on the bulletin board.

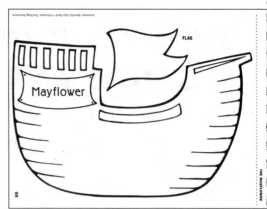

★ PILGRIM LIFE

Stock your class library with a variety of books about Pilgrims. Then have students use the books, along with other sources, such as the Internet and videos, to learn about Pilgrim life in Plymouth, Massachusetts. For example, instruct students to find out about the Pilgrims' homes, diets, survival skills, and the different roles of the adults and children. After discussing, invite individuals, partners, or small groups to create posters or books about Pilgrim life. They can use photocopies of the Pilgrim characters (pages 94 and 95) as part of their projects. Or, you might enlarge the characters and display with students' projects on a bulletin board. (Enlist volunteers to color the characters for the display.)

★ DRESSED FOR THE DAY

Display pictures of Pilgrim children and describe their clothing. Name some of the articles of clothing that the girls wore, such as a petticoat, waistcoat, apron, coif, and stockings. Then name some of the boys' clothing: breeches, doublet, points, stockings, and hat. Afterward, invite students to make Pilgrim headwear that they can wear when presenting their Pilgrim-related projects, telling stories about Pilgrim life, or role-playing the Thanksgiving story. Have students follow the directions below to make the headwear of their choice.

Coif

Pilgrim girls wore a head covering called a coif. Provide students with 12- by 18-inch sheets of construction paper and tape. Then have each student who wishes to make a coif do the following:

1. Fold the paper into thirds and crease lightly.

2. Unfold the paper and cut a notch along each fold line, as shown.

3. Fold up the bottom edge opposite the notched edge.

4. Bring the top corners of the paper back so that the straight edges meet to form a loop. Tape in place.

5. Bend the top edge of the center section toward the back to give the coif a dome-like shape. Secure with tape.

6. Attach yarn ties to each side of the coif.

Hat

While most Pilgrim boys wore simple hats (metal buckles were not common at that time), students who make this hat may opt to add a decorative buckle. To make hats, have students cut out a hat shape from 9- by 12-inch sheets of construction paper, as shown. They can add a brown band above the brim, and a yellow buckle, if desired. Then have students add a 1- by 12-inch strip of black paper to each side of their hat. Help them fit the hat to their head and staple the ends in place.

★ THE WAMPANOAGS

The Wampanoags befriended the Pilgrims and helped them in many ways, although the lifestyles of the two groups were very different. Have students do research to learn about the Wampanoags—their homes, way of life, methods of food gathering, clothing, and so on. Students can create posters, murals, books, skits, and songs as ways to communicate their findings. Then invite them to do the following to make paper-bag vests:

(continued)

1. Cut an opening up the front panel of a large paper bag, as shown. Then cut out a neck hole and armholes. Fringe the bottom edge of the bag.

2. Use crayons, colored markers, or paint to create designs and symbols on the vest. (If the bag has print on it, carefully turn it inside out and decorate the plain side.)

3. Wear the vest to present Wampanoag-related projects or for dramatizations and story telling.

4. If desired, make a feathered headband from construction paper to wear with the vest.

 ## THANKSGIVING PUPPETS AND PROPS

Invite students to make these puppets and props to use in their Thanksgiving-related presentations, dramatizations, story telling, and so on:

Thanksgiving Finger Puppets

To make these quick-and-easy finger puppets, photocopy the puppet patterns (page 96) for each student. Then have students color and cut out their puppets. Help them, as needed, to cut out the small circles on the puppet. To use, students simply slip their fingers into the holes and wiggle them around to serve as legs for their Pilgrim and Wampanoag characters. Encourage students to act out the first Thanksgiving with their finger puppets.

Stand-Up Characters

Distribute photocopies of the Thanksgiving character patterns on pages 97–100. Ask students to color and cut out each pattern. Then have them bring each character's hands together and glue the object for that character between his or her hands. (The Pilgrim girl will hold a pie, the Pilgrim boy a turkey, the Wampanoag girl a basket of corn, and the Wampanoag boy a pumpkin.) Finally, fold back each side of the cutouts and stand on a flat surface.

Wampanoag Picture Props

Photocopy and distribute the Wampanoag characters on page 101. Have students color and cut out the characters for use as props when sharing what they know about these people or in telling stories about the first Thanksgiving.

★ A HARVEST OF THANKSGIVING FACTS

While Thanksgiving Day is viewed in the United States as a uniquely American holiday, many cultures around the world have long-standing traditions of celebrating their harvest with a time of thanksgiving. Corn was a staple of the Pilgrims' diet, but they also grew other plants, such as squash and beans. To create a crop of Thanksgiving facts, attach long strips of green paper to a bulletin board to represent corn stalks. Next, distribute photocopies of the patterns on pages 102 and 103. (You might copy the ear of corn on yellow paper and the leaf and husk on green paper.) Then have students do the following:

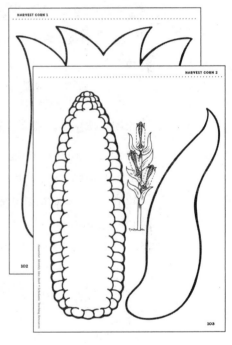

1. Cut out the patterns.

2. Write a Thanksgiving fact on the ear of corn. Or, write about an event relating to the Pilgrims or Wampanoags.

3. Glue the corn to the middle of the husk. Fold the sides of the husk over the corn.

4. Attach the corn and leaf cutout to a stalk, as shown.

5. To use, open the corn husks and read the facts on the corn.

★ HORN OF PLENTY

Review some of the plant foods that the Pilgrims and early settlers enjoyed. Then invite students to make a cornucopia, or "horn of plenty," to commemorate the first Thanksgiving. To begin, distribute photocopies of the food patterns on pages 104 and 105 and the cornucopia on page 106. Ask students to color and cut out their patterns. Then have them carefully cut out the center of the cornucopia. To fill their cornucopia, students can glue their foods along the edges of the opening of the cornucopia and glue some of the foods to each other. Have them overlap

(continued)

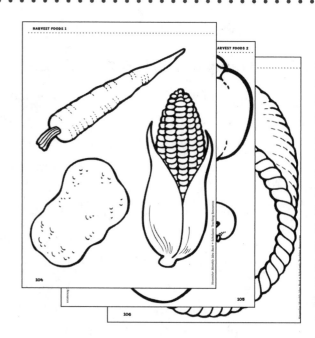

the cutouts to fit them over the opening, in front of, and to the sides of their cornucopia so that the foods appear to be spilling out. If desired, students can glue their completed cornucopias to a colorful sheet of construction paper. Alternately, students can write something they are thankful for on the back of each food cutout, then tape the foods to their cornucopia, making sure each food can be lifted up to read the text on the back. You might also enlarge the food and cornucopia patterns to use for a class display.

CREATIVE WRITING FOR THANKSGIVING

Encourage students to do some Thanksgiving-related creative writing with the following ideas.

Thanksgiving Stationery

Discuss with students the many things that the Pilgrims gave thanks for on that first Thanksgiving. Then encourage them to reflect on things that they are most thankful for. Invite volunteers to share their thoughts. Afterward, give students photocopies of their choice of the stationery on pages 107 and 108. Have them write about what they are thankful for. If students chose the stationery on page 108, they might write a list in the opening of the cornucopia, then compose a poem, rhyme, or song on the lines.

Turkey Story Starters

Cut out photocopies of the turkey patterns on pages 109–110. Post the cutouts in a center, then have students write a story, using the text on one of the turkeys as a story starter. Or, copy enough of the turkeys so that you have one for each student. Distribute the cutouts to students and have them write about the situation described on their turkey. Later, invite students to share their completed stories with the class.

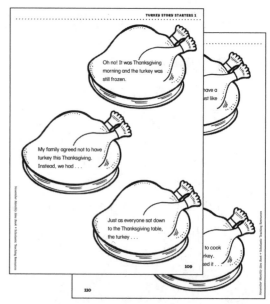

My Turkey Recipe

Distribute photocopies of page 111 to students and have them write their own turkey recipes. The recipes can be realistic, based on watching or helping someone prepare a turkey. Or, students might write recipes for imaginary or silly ways to prepare a Thanksgiving turkey. Invite volunteers to share their recipes with the class, then display them on a bulletin board or bind them into a class book for all to enjoy.

★ GOBBLE, GOBBLE! PAGE TOPPER

This "hungry" turkey page topper adds fun and flair to students' Thanksgiving-related writing assignments. Distribute photocopies of the turkey pattern on page 112. Have students color and cut out the pattern, then glue their cutout to the top of a sheet of construction paper. Students can attach their written work (or other work, such as Thanksgiving drawings) to the construction paper. If desired, enlarge the pattern onto poster board. Color and cut out the turkey, then laminate for durability. You can mount the cutout over the top of a bulletin board filled with students' work. Or, place it over your classroom door to welcome visitors to a Thanksgiving feast hosted by your class (see below).

★ A THANKSGIVING FEAST

To wrap up your studies, plan a Thanksgiving feast for your class. (Or, plan the feast with several other classes.) To prepare, send home notes asking parents and caregivers to bring in foods or dishes eaten during Pilgrim times. You might send home a list of foods from which they can make their selections. On the list, include foods such as nuts, pumpkin seeds, dried cranberries, popcorn, currants or raisins, corn, and beans. You also might include recipes from sources such as *Eating the Plates* by Lucille Recht Penner and *The Thanksgiving Primer* by Plimouth Plantation Publications. Request that families let you know in advance which foods they plan to contribute to the feast. (Always check for food allergies or sensitivity issues when serving food in class.) On the day of the feast, have students help set up and decorate tables with Thanksgiving centerpieces, napkins rings, and so on. Then enjoy the feast and company of your students and their families.

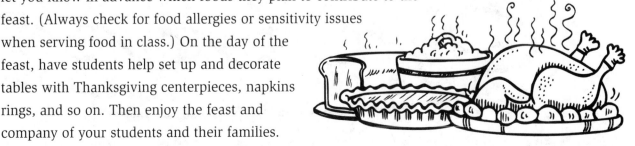

PLACE THIS SIDE ALONG FOLD.

Mayflower

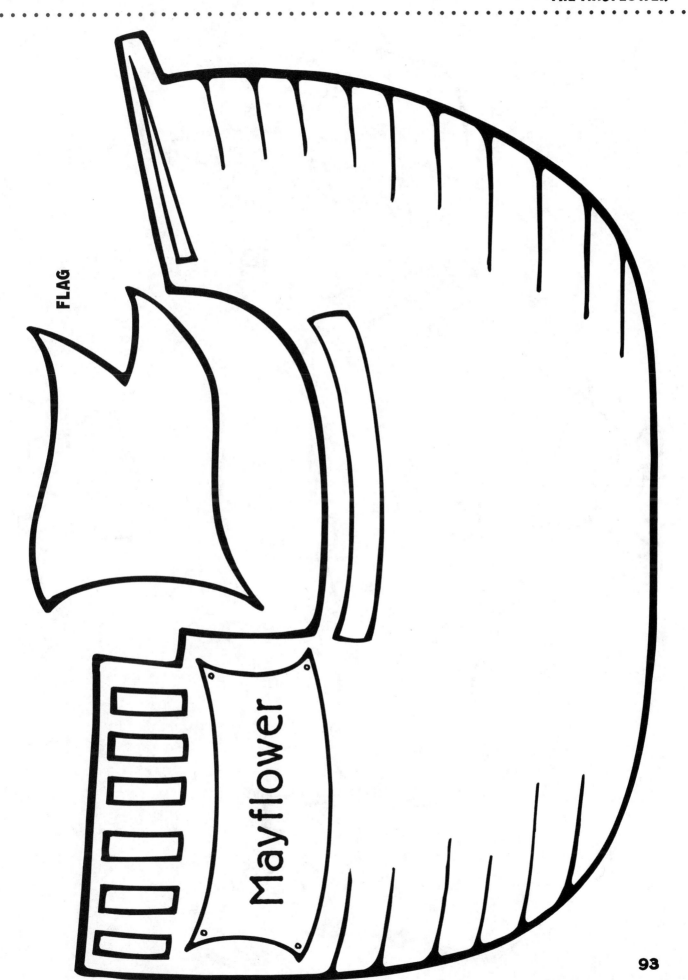

FLAG

Mayflower

Cut out. Cut out.

Cut out. Cut out.

Cut out. Cut out.

Cut out. Cut out.

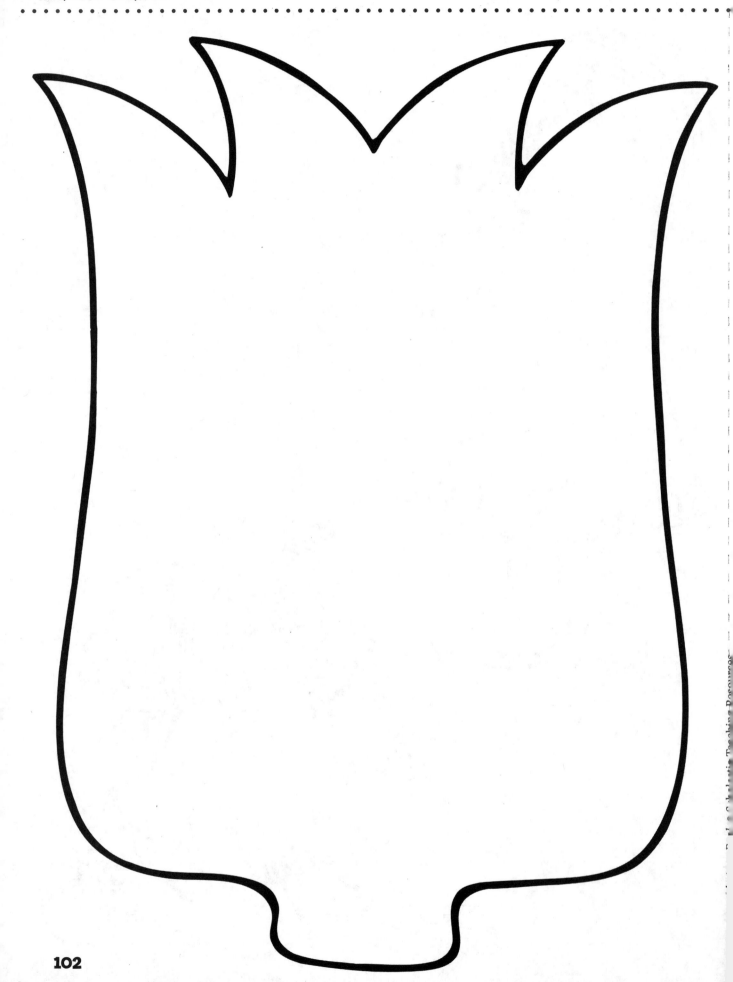

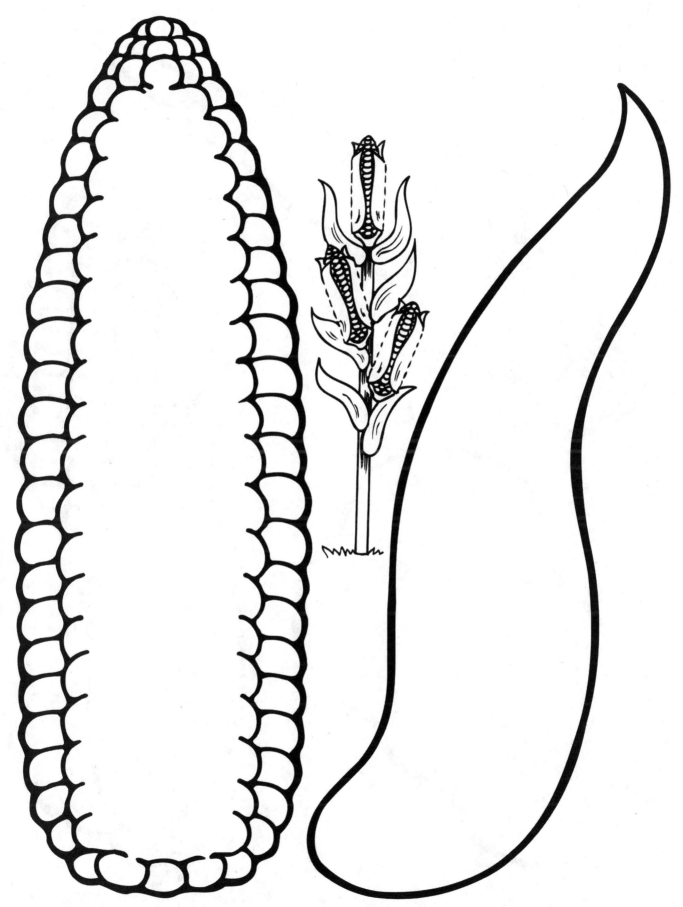

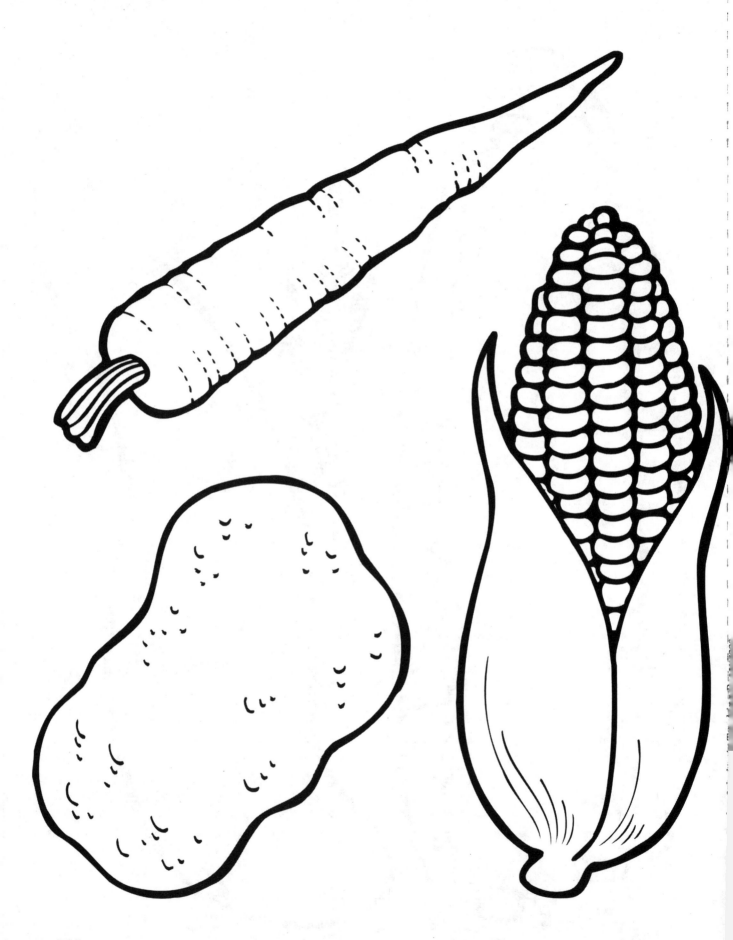

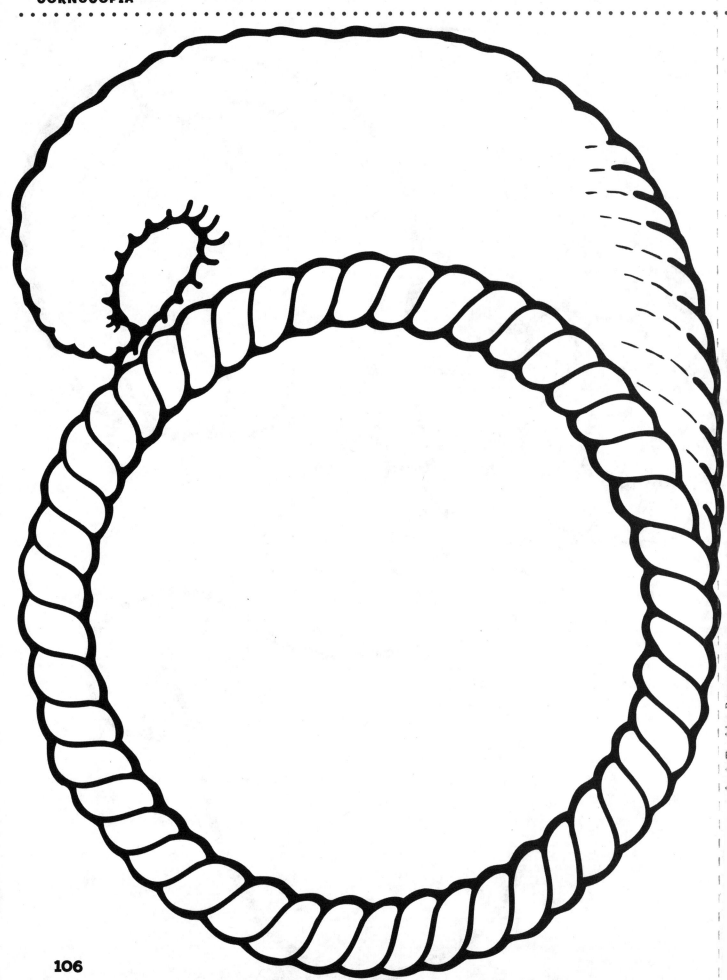

I am thankful for . . .

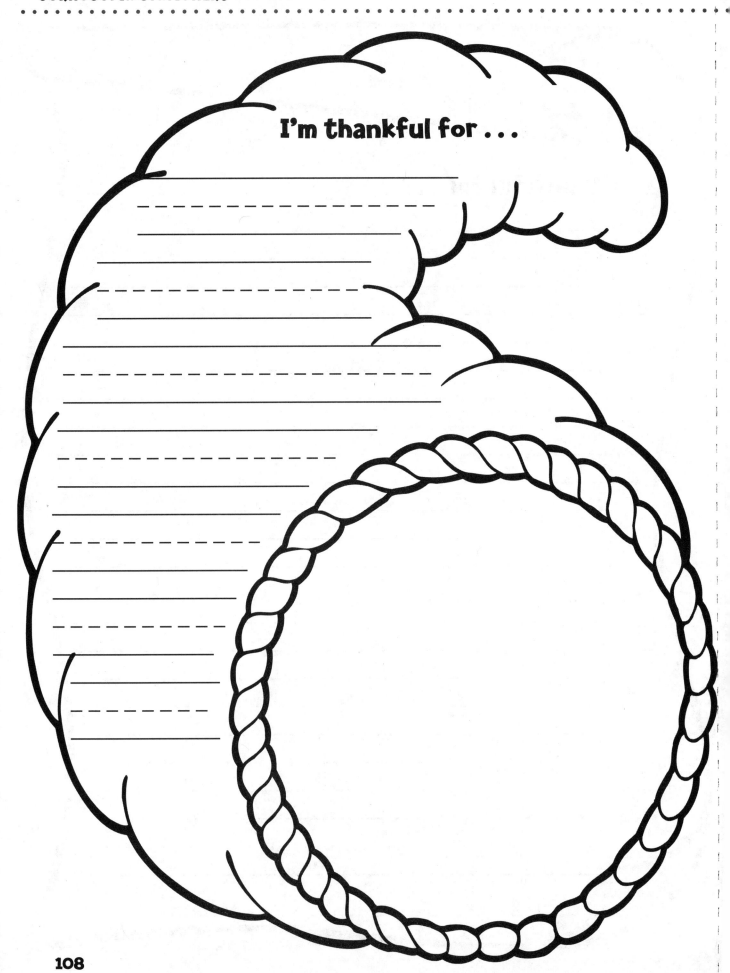

I'm thankful for . . .

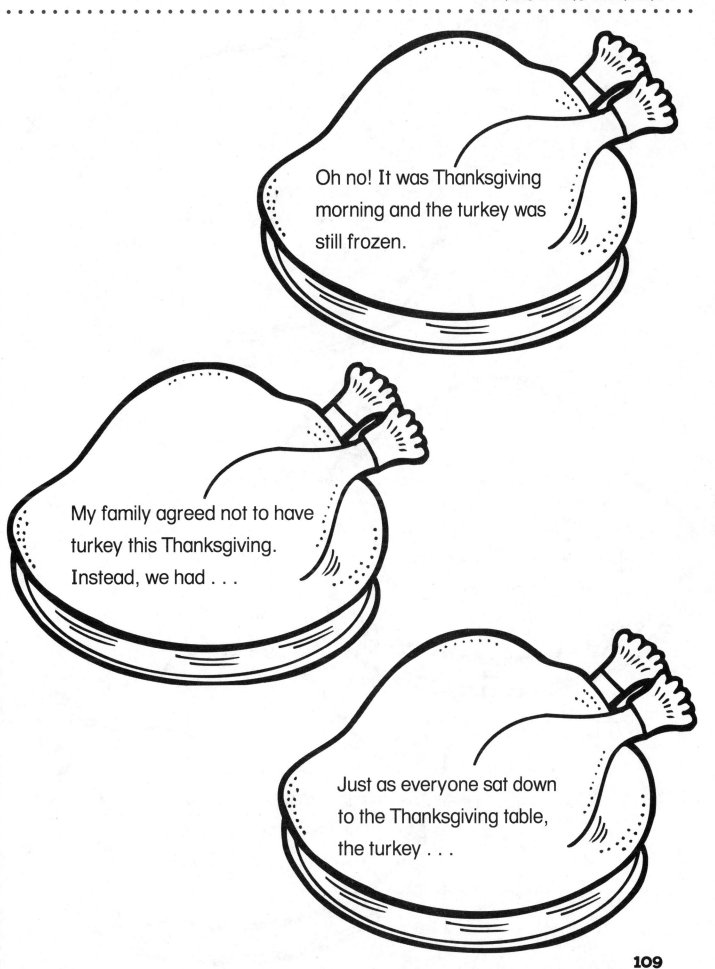

Oh no! It was Thanksgiving morning and the turkey was still frozen.

My family agreed not to have turkey this Thanksgiving. Instead, we had . . .

Just as everyone sat down to the Thanksgiving table, the turkey . . .

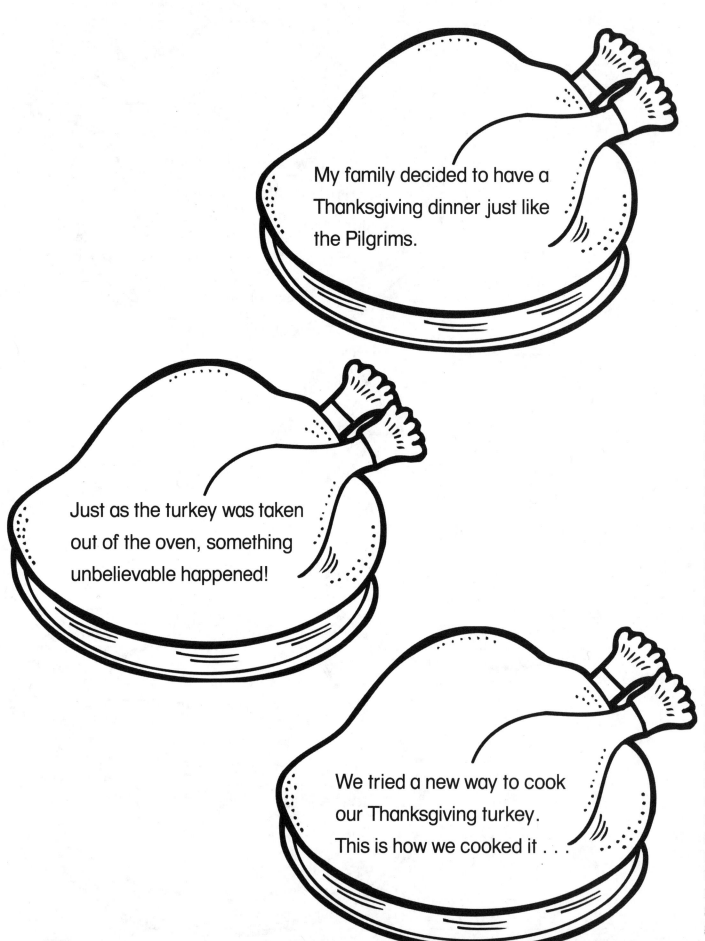

My family decided to have a Thanksgiving dinner just like the Pilgrims.

Just as the turkey was taken out of the oven, something unbelievable happened!

We tried a new way to cook our Thanksgiving turkey. This is how we cooked it . . .

My Turkey Recipe

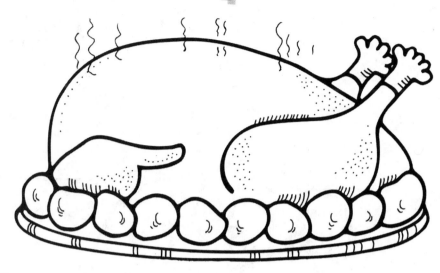

Ingredients:

_____   _____

_____   _____

_____   _____

_____   _____

Directions: _____

_____

_____

_____

_____

Cooking Time: _____

Oven Temperature: _____

TURKEY TIME!

The North American wild turkey was native to our land long before the arrival of the Pilgrims. These birds, which looked somewhat different from the images of domestic turkeys we see today, were a vital source of food and clothing for many of the East Coast natives.

Male turkeys are called *toms* and females are *hens*. Turkey eggs have cream-colored or tan shells with brown specks and are about twice as large as chicken eggs. The young turkeys that hatch are called *poults*. Unlike many domestic turkeys that are grown for food, wild turkeys are smaller and weigh only about ten pounds. Wild turkeys also have darker feathers and can fly. In fact, many fly onto tree branches where they perch overnight.

Suggested Activities

★ ALL ABOUT TURKEYS

Share the information about turkeys from the introduction above. Then invite students to share additional facts they know about turkeys. Afterward, have them do research to learn more about this interesting bird. Students might choose to research wild turkeys or domestic turkeys. Explain that they can use classroom, library, and Internet resources as well as videos, personal interviews, and other helpful sources to gather information about turkeys. Distribute photocopies of the stationery on page 118 for students to use to write the final draft of their findings. Then they can compile their pages into a book, using photocopies of page 119 to prepare a cover for their written work.

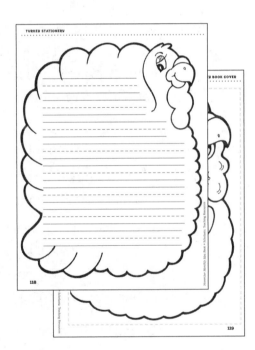

★ MR. TURKEY PAGE FRAMER

Turkeys are fascinating animals that are sure to inspire students' imagination and creativity. Encourage students to write short stories, skits, poems, songs, or other text about turkeys. Or, have them draw imaginative pictures or cartoons of these creatures. When students complete their work, distribute photocopies of the

(continued)

turkey patterns on pages 120–121. To make the page framer, ask students to color and cut out the patterns, then glue the turkey's head, wings, and feet to the edges of a sheet of construction paper, as shown. Finally, have them attach their written work or drawing to the front of the page framer.

 ## FEATHER-FRIEND FACTS

Students can make the following projects to share and show off their turkey knowledge. You might display the completed projects on a bulletin board or in a designated area of the room or hallway.

Hinged Fact Turkey

Fill up a class bulletin board with these friendly turkeys stuffed with facts. For each student, photocopy pages 122 and 123 once and page 124 twice. Distribute a set of turkey patterns and four brass fasteners to each student. Then have students do the following to make their turkeys:

1. Color and cut out the patterns.

2. Write a turkey fact on the body. If desired, write additional facts on the wings and tail feathers.

3. Use the paper fasteners to assemble the turkey, as shown. (Stack the feathers and use one brass fastener to attach them to the turkey.)

You might also display students' written work about turkeys or Thanksgiving with these beautiful birds!

Turkey Feather Facts

For each student, photocopy the turkey and two or three sets of the feathers (pages 125–126). You might copy the feathers onto yellow, orange, red, and light brown construction paper. Have students cut out their patterns and write a turkey fact on each one. Then invite them to color their turkey and feathers (if not on colored paper).

Finally, to assemble, have students glue the feathers to the back of their turkey. As an alternative, you might have students label each feather with a turkey- or Thanksgiving-related book that they have read. Or, they might write about things they are thankful for on the turkey and feathers.

★ TURKEY PAPER-BAG PUPPET

Invite students to make puppets to use for their turkey role-playing and dramatizations. To begin, distribute a small paper bag and a photocopy of the turkey patterns on page 127 to each student. Also, provide a supply of construction paper in assorted colors. Then have students do the following to make their puppets:

1. Color and cut out the patterns.

2. Glue the turkey's head to the bottom flap of the bag. Glue its mouth to the front of the bag just under the flap.

3. Cut out a few colorful construction-paper feathers and glue to the back of the bag.

4. If desired, write a few turkey facts on the paper bag.

★ HANDS-DOWN TURKEY

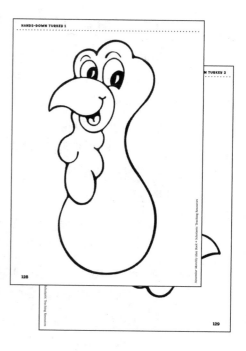

This delightful turkey display will be a hands-down class favorite! First, enlarge the turkey head and feet patterns (pages 128–129) onto poster board. Color and cut out the body parts. Then have students work with partners to trace their hands and feet onto red, yellow, brown, and orange sheets of construction paper. When finished, ask them to cut out their outlines. Then use the turkey patterns and the hand and foot cutouts to fashion a turkey on a bulletin board, as shown. If desired, display students' turkey- or Thanksgiving-related stories or illustrations around the turkey.

115

★ TURKEY CENTERPIECE

This potato turkey makes the perfect
centerpiece for any Thanksgiving dinner
table. To prepare, photocopy a class supply
of the turkey patterns on pages 130–131.
Distribute the patterns, a small potato,
and several flat wooden toothpicks to each
student. (In advance, you might cut a small,
flat spot on the bottom of each potato to
keep it from rolling.) Have students color
and cut out their patterns. Then instruct
them to fold the turkey head along the
line where indicated. To attach the head, wings, and tail to the
potato (the body), help students poke a toothpick through each
body part and into the potato, as shown. (If needed, break the
toothpicks into shorter lengths before inserting them.)

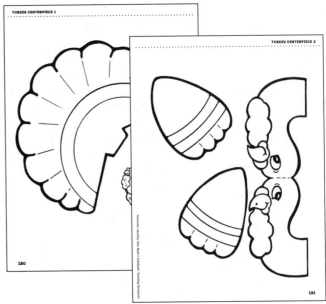

To make a larger class turkey centerpiece, enlarge the patterns,
have students help prepare them, then attach the turkey cutouts to
a pumpkin body.

★ TURKEY NAPKIN RING

Invite students to make these napkin rings to add to their
Thanksgiving table setting. Students can tuck a napkin into
the rings, or slip in rolled pieces of paper labeled with turkey
or Thanksgiving facts. To begin, photocopy the patterns on
page 132 and distribute to students, along with 2-inch lengths
of cardboard tubes. Have them do the following to make their
napkin ring:

1. Color and cut out the turkey head and feathers. Also,
   color the cardboard tube.

2. Fold the turkey head where indicated. Then fold out the
   tabs and glue to the tube.

3. Fold up the tab on the tail and glue to the opposite
   side of the tube, as shown.

TURKEY SKILLS WHEEL

Use the turkey wheel patterns on pages 133–134 to reinforce math skills and more. To prepare, write a problem in each of the large boxes (outlined in gray). Write the answer in the small box directly opposite each problem on the left. Cut out the turkey, wing, and wheel. Then carefully cut out the "windows" on the turkey. Use one brass fastener to attach the wheel to the turkey and another to attach the wing, as shown. To use, students turn the wheel so that a problem appears in the right window. They solve the problem and then slide the wing away from the left window to check their answer.

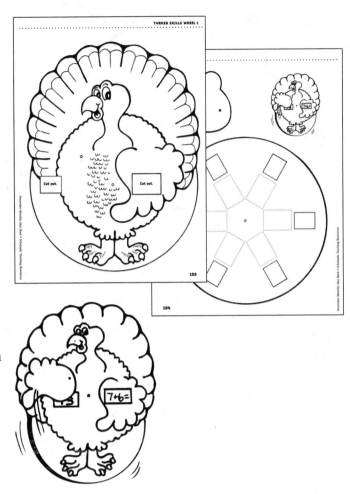

 ## STRUTTIN' ALONG FUN GLASSES

Invite students to make and wear a pair of turkey glasses for fun or as a prop when presenting their turkey-related projects. Distribute photocopies of the glasses patterns on page 135. Have students color and cut out the patterns, carefully cutting the slits on the glasses frame and the earpieces. To assemble, students simply fit each earpiece into the corresponding slit on the frame. If desired, students can take their glasses home to share with family members.

PLACE THIS SIDE ALONG FOLD.

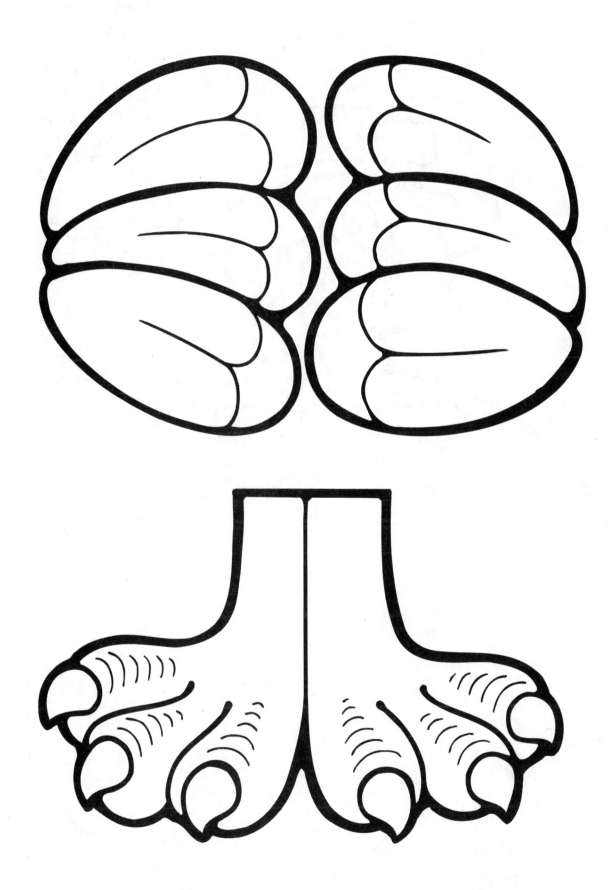

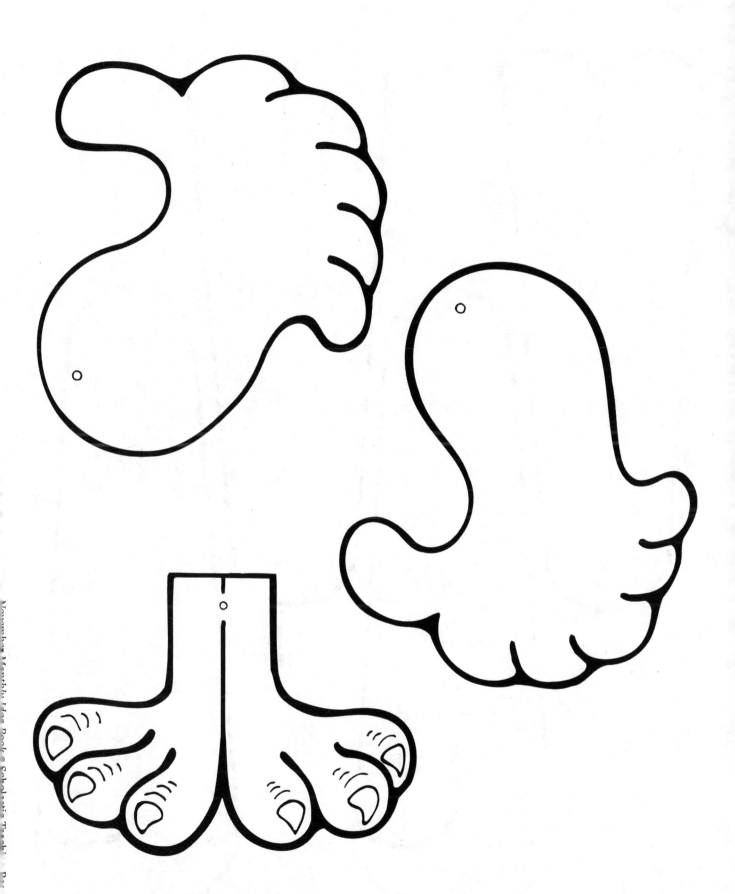

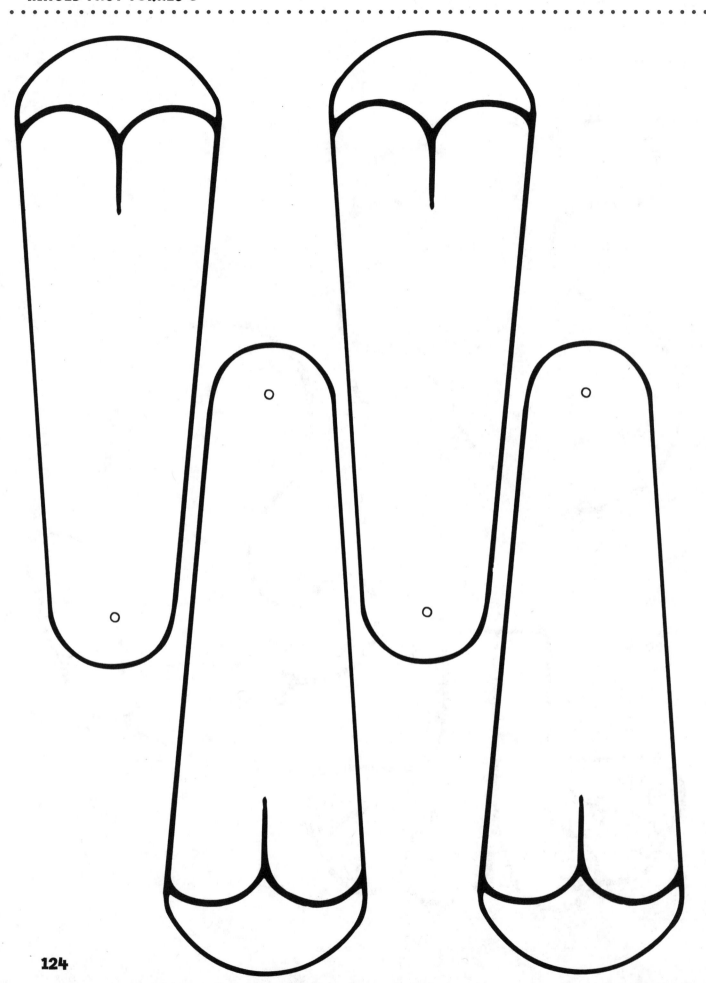

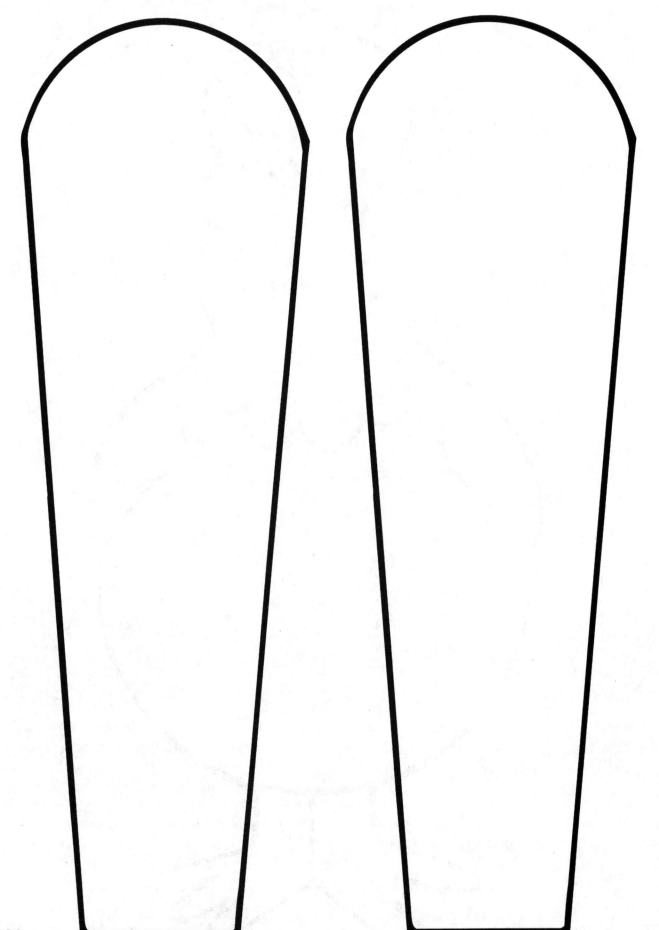

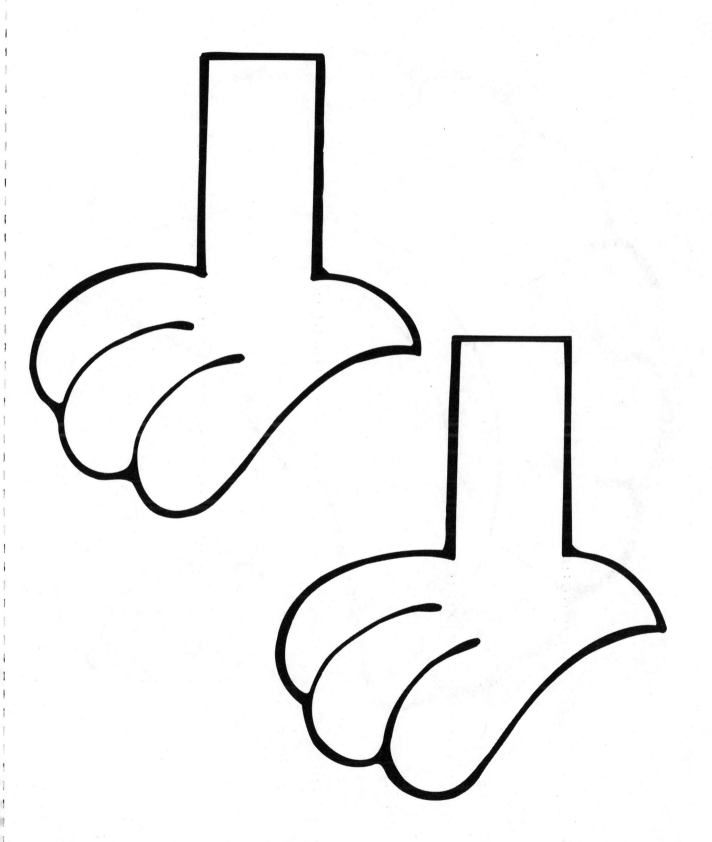

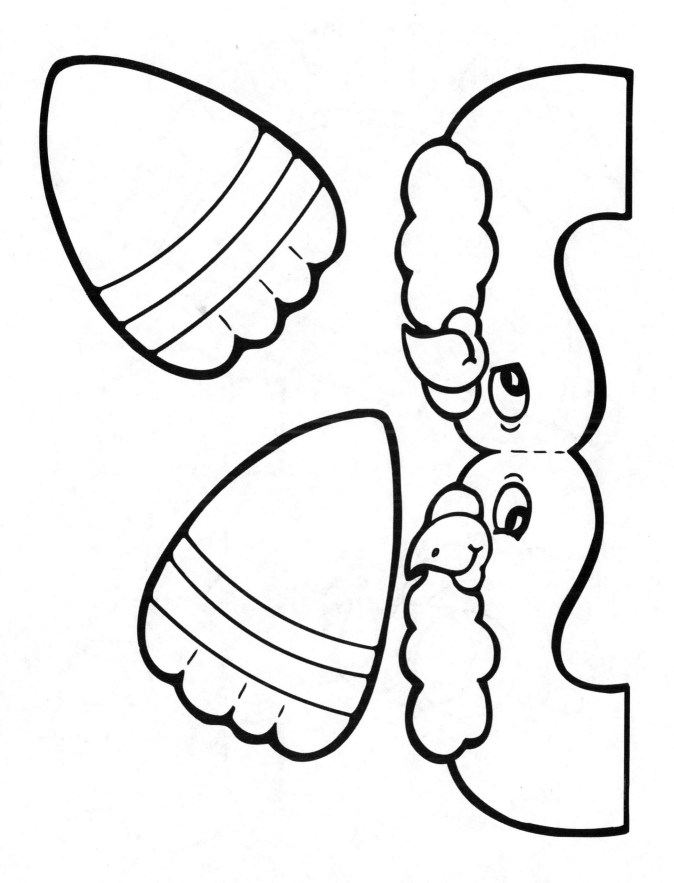

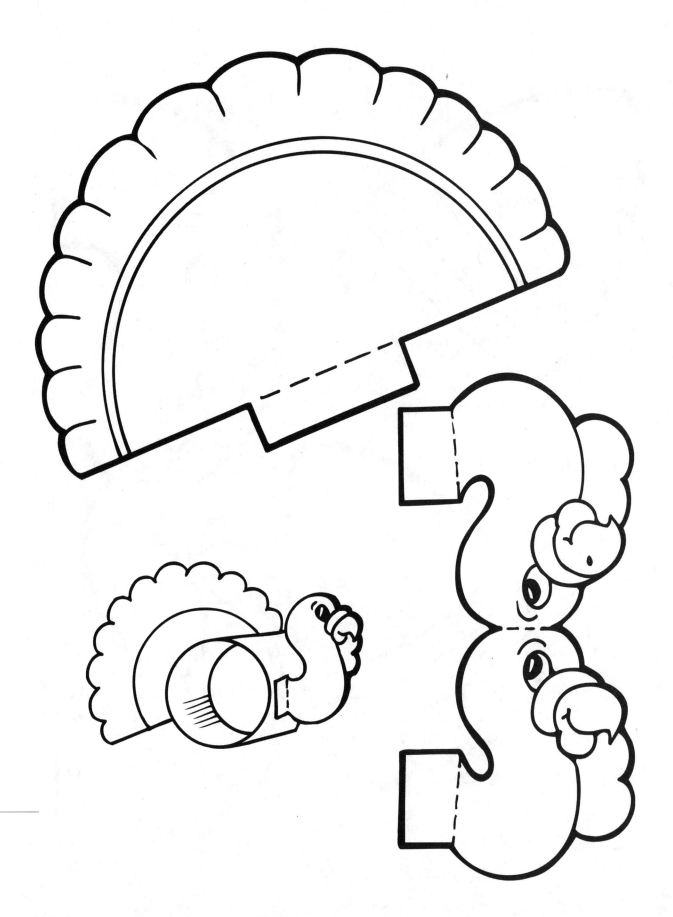

Cut out.

Cut out.

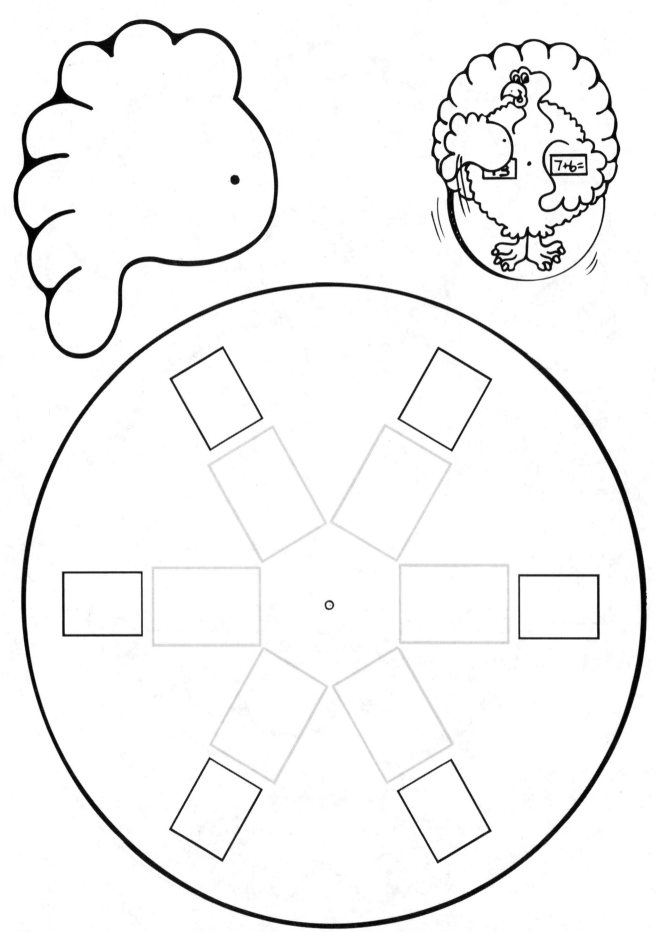

7+6=

AWARDS, INCENTIVES, AND MORE

Getting Started

Make several photocopies of the reproducibles on pages 138 through 142. Giving out the bookmarks, pencil toppers, notes, and certificates will show students your enthusiasm for their efforts and achievements. Plus, bookmarks and pencil toppers are a fun treat for students celebrating birthdays.

■ Provide materials for decorating, including markers, color pencils, and stickers.

■ Encourage students to bring home their creations to show and celebrate with family members.

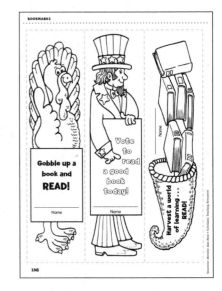

★ BOOKMARKS

1. Photocopy onto tagboard and cut apart.

2. For more fanfare, punch a hole on one end and tie on a length of colorful ribbon or yarn.

★ PENCIL TOPPERS

1. Photocopy onto tagboard and cut out.

2. Use an art knife to cut through the Xs.

3. Slide a pencil through the Xs as shown.

SEND-HOME NOTES

1. Photocopy and cut apart.

2. Record the child's name and the date.

3. Add your signature.

4. Add more details about the student's day on the back of the note.

 CERTIFICATES

1. Photocopy.

2. Record the child's name and other information, as directed.

3. Add details about the child's achievement (if applicable), then add your signature and date.

**Gobble up a
book and
READ!**

_____
Name

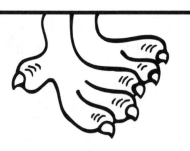

**Vote
to
read
a good
book
today!**

_____
Name

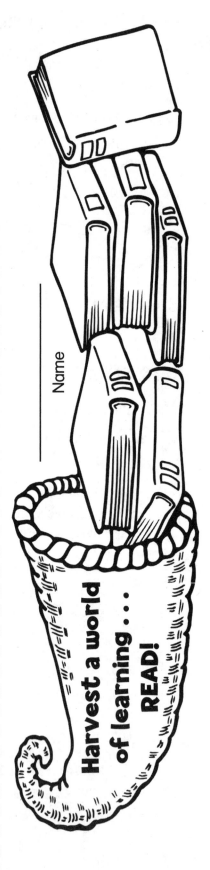

**Harvest a world
of learning . . .
READ!**

_____
Name

_____
Student's Name

harvested some healthy learning today!

Teacher   Date

Gobble! Gobble!

Much Better!

_____
Student's Name

Teacher   Date

_____
Student's Name

really did a great job today!

Teacher   Date

WOW!

Look who was a terrific student today!

_____
Student's Name

Teacher   Date

Student of the Week

Name

School

Teacher

Date

Certificate of Achievement

presented to

Name

in recognition of

Teacher

Date

Election Word Find, page 43

```
S V R T G H Y K L H N(S P E E C H)F B N K L Y
X Z A S W Q R T H Y(B)H R D C V T Y H U J M H
D C X V(C A N D I D A T E)F H J(I)I L K M N G
V F G H O S X V B H L J S F T Y(N A T I O N)P
W R T Y N C H Y U I L N I B G H A R Y U I O P
C V G Y V H U I K J O R D S W E U C V(C)W Q E
Q S X D E G B F D R T U E D S W G F R A F V B
M L K O(N O V E M B E R)N O K J U J K M F G T
(E L E C T I O N)D R T Y T H N J R H G P C V B
R T Y U I S R T G H U J K I O L A G H A C X Z
L P O I O G F(D E M O C R A T)F T A W I D R T
S G H U(N)G H Y U I K M N H U Y I F T G E W Y
(V I C E P R E S I D E N T)F G T O F N N C E T
O F R H G B N M K I L O H B G Y N R F D E W S
(T E R M)C D F(R E P U B L I C A N)F R H Y U K
(E)S C V T G B N J U I K M K L O P M N J H Y T
X D R T G V B H U J M N H Y T R E W Q A S D E
F R G B N J I U H J K L O P M N B V G F R Q W
```

Name That State!, page 54

1. Washington
2. Oregon
3. California
4. Nevada
5. Idaho
6. Arizona
7. Utah
8. Montana
9. Wyoming
10. Colorado
11. New Mexico
12. North Dakota
13. South Dakota
14. Nebraska
15. Kansas
16. Oklahoma
17. Texas
18. Minnesota
19. Iowa
20. Missouri
21. Arkansas
22. Louisiana
23. Wisconsin
24. Illinois
25. Michigan
26. Indiana
27. Kentucky
28. Tennessee
29. Mississippi
30. Alabama
31. Ohio
32: West Virginia
33. Virginia
34. North Carolina
35. South Carolina
36. Georgia
37. Florida
38. Pennsylvania
39. New York
40. Vermont
41. New Hampshire
42. Maine
43. Massachusetts
44. Connecticut
45. Rhode Island
46. New Jersey
47. Delaware
48. Maryland
49. Alaska
50. Hawaii

What Is the Capital?, page 55

Alabama	Montgomery
Alaska	Juneau
Arizona	Phoenix
Arkansas	Little Rock
California	Sacramento
Colorado	Denver
Connecticut	Hartford
Delaware	Dover
Florida	Tallahassee
Georgia	Atlanta
Hawaii	Honolulu
Idaho	Boise
Illinois	Springfield
Indiana	Indianapolis
Iowa	Des Moines
Kansas	Topeka
Kentucky	Frankfort
Louisiana	Baton Rouge
Maine	Augusta
Maryland	Annapolis
Massachusetts	Boston
Michigan	Lansing
Minnesota	Saint Paul
Mississippi	Jackson
Missouri	Jefferson City
Montana	Helena
Nebraska	Lincoln
Nevada	Carson City
New Hampshire	Concord
New Jersey	Trenton
New Mexico	Santa Fe
New York	Albany
North Carolina	Raleigh
North Dakota	Bismarck
Ohio	Columbus
Oklahoma	Oklahoma City
Oregon	Salem
Pennsylvania	Harrisburg
Rhode Island	Providence
South Carolina	Columbia
South Dakota	Pierre
Tennessee	Nashville
Texas	Austin
Utah	Salt Lake City
Vermont	Montpelier
Virginia	Richmond
Washington	Olympia
West Virginia	Charleston
Wisconsin	Madison
Wyoming	Cheyenne

NOTES